Ivan Sergeevich Turgenev, William Hand Browne, Sophie Michell
Butts

Ïvan Turgénieff's Spring floods

Ivan Sergeevich Turgenev, William Hand Browne, Sophie Michell Butts

Ïvan Turgénieff's Spring floods

ISBN/EAN: 9783337113650

Printed in Europe, USA, Canada, Australia, Japan

Cover: Foto ©ninafisch / pixelio.de

More available books at **www.hansebooks.com**

SMOKE

A Novel

BY

IVAN TURGENEV

Translated from the Russian
By CONSTANCE GARNETT

LARGE TYPE FINE-PAPER EDITION

LONDON
WILLIAM HEINEMANN
1914

First Edition, 1896.
New Impressions, 1901, 1904, 1905.
Large Type Fine-paper Edition, 1907.
New Impressions, 1910, 1914.

LOAN STACK

[*All rights reserved*]

INTRODUCTION

'SMOKE' was first published in 1867, several years after Turgenev had fixed his home in Baden, with his friends the Viardots. Baden at this date was a favourite resort for all circles of Russian society, and Turgenev was able to study at his leisure his countrymen as they appeared to foreign critical eyes. The novel is therefore the most cosmopolitan of all Turgenev's works. On a veiled background of the great world of European society, little groups of representative Russians, members of the aristocratic and the Young Russia parties, are etched with an incisive, unfaltering hand. *Smoke*, as an historical study, though it yields in importance to *Fathers and Children* and *Virgin Soil*, is of great significance to Russians. It might with truth have been named *Transition*, for the generation it paints was then midway between the early philosophical Nihilism of the sixties and the active political Nihilism of the seventies.

Markedly transitional, however, as was the Russian mind of the days of *Smoke*, Turgenev, with the faculty that distinguishes the great artist from the artist of second rank, the faculty of seeking out and stamping the essential under confused and fleeting forms, has once and for ever laid bare the fundamental weakness of the Slav nature, its weakness of will. *Smoke* is an attack, a deserved attack, not merely on the Young Russia Party, but on all the Parties; not on the old ideas or the new ideas, but on the proneness of the Slav nature to fall a prey to a consuming weakness, a moral stagnation, a feverish *ennui*, the Slav nature that analyses everything with force and brilliancy, and ends, so often, by doing nothing. *Smoke* is the attack, bitter yet sympathetic, of a man who, with growing despair, has watched the weakness of his countrymen, while he loves his country all the more for the bitterness their sins have brought upon it. *Smoke* is the scourging of a babbling generation, by a man who, grown sick to death of the chatter of reformers and reactionists, is visiting the sins of the fathers on the children, with a contempt out of patience for the hereditary vice in the Slav blood. And this time the author cannot be accused of partisanship by any blunderer. 'A plague o' both your houses,' is his message equally to the Bureaucrats and the Revolutionists. And so skilfully does he wield the thong, that every lash falls on the back of both parties. An exquisite piece of political satire is *Smoke*; for this reason alone it would stand unique among novels.

The success of *Smoke* was immediate and great; but the hue-and-cry that assailed it was even greater. The publication of the book marks the final rupture between Turgenev and the party of Young Russia. The younger generation never forgave him for drawing Gubaryov and Bambaev, Voroshilov and Madame Suhantchikov—types, indeed, in which all revolutionary or unorthodox parties are painfully rich. Or, perhaps, Turgenev was forgiven for it when he was in his grave, a spot where forgiveness flowers to a late perfection. And yet the fault was not Turgenev's. No, his last novel, *Virgin Soil*, bears splendid witness that it was Young Russia that was one-eyed.

Let the plain truth here be set down. *Smoke*

is not a complete picture of the Young Russia of the day; it was not yet time for that picture; and that being so, Turgenev did the next best thing in attacking the windbags, the charlatans and their crowd of shallow, chattering followers, as well as the empty formulas of the *laissez-faire* party. It was inevitable that the attack should bring on him the anger of all young enthusiasts working for 'the Cause'; it was inevitable that 'the Cause' of reform in Russia should be mixed up with the Gubaryovs, just as reforms in France a few years ago were mixed up with Boulanger; and that Turgenev's waning popularity for the last twenty years of his life should be directly caused by his honesty and clear-sightedness in regard to Russian Liberalism, was inevitable also. To be crucified by those you have benefited is the cross of honour of all great, single-hearted men.

But though the bitterness of political life flavours *Smoke*, although its points of departure and arrival are wrapped in the atmosphere of Russia's dark and insoluble problems, nevertheless the two central figures of the book, Litvinov and Irina, are not political figures. Luckily for them, in Gubaryov's words, they belong 'to the undeveloped.' Litvinov himself may be dismissed in a sentence. He is Turgenev's favourite type of man, a character much akin to his own nature, gentle, deep, and sympathetic. Turgenev often drew such a character; Lavretsky, for example, in *A House of Gentlefolk*, is a first cousin to Litvinov, an older and a sadder man.

But Irina—Irina is unique; for Turgenev has in her perfected her type till she reaches a destroying witchery of fascination and subtlety. Irina will stand for ever in the long gallery of great creations, smiling with that enigmatical smile which took from Litvinov in a glance half his life, and his love for Tatyana. The special triumph of her creation is that she combines that exact balance between good and evil which makes good women seem insipid beside her and bad women unnatural. And, by nature irresistible, she is made doubly so to the imagination by the situation which she recreates between Litvinov and herself. She ardently desires to become nobler, to possess all that the ideal of love means for the heart of woman; but she has only the power given to her of enervating the man she loves. Can she become a Tatyana to him? No, to no man. She is born to corrupt, yet never to be corrupted. She rises mistress of herself after the first measure of fatal delight. And, never giving her whole heart absolutely to her lover, she, nevertheless, remains ever to be desired.

Further, her wit, her scorn, her beauty preserve her from all the influences of evil she does not deliberately employ. Such a woman is as old and as rare a type as Helen of Troy. It is most often found among the great mistresses of princes, and it was from a mistress of Alexander II. that Turgenev modelled Irina.

Of the minor characters, Tatyana is an astonishing instance of Turgenev's skill in drawing a complete character with half-a-dozen strokes of the pen. The reader seems to have known her intimately all his life: her family life, her girlhood, her goodness and individual ways to the smallest detail; yet she only speaks on two or three occasions. Potugin is but a weary shadow of Litvinov, but it is difficult to say how much this is a telling refinement of art. The shadow of this prematurely exhausted man is cast beforehand by Irina across Litvinov's future. For Turgenev to have drawn

INTRODUCTION

Potugin as an ordinary individual would have vulgarised the novel and robbed it of its skilful proportions, for Potugin is one of those shadowy figures which supply the chiaroscuro to a brilliant etching.

As a triumphant example of consummate technical skill, *Smoke* will repay the most exact scrutiny. There are a lightness and a grace about the novel that conceal its actual strength. The political argument glides with such ease in and out of the love story, that the hostile critic is absolutely baffled; and while the most intricate steps are executed in the face of a crowd of angry enemies, the performer lands smiling and in safety. The art by which Irina's disastrous fascination results in falsity, and Litvinov's desperate striving after sincerity ends in rehabilitation,—the art by which these two threads are spun, till their meaning colours the faint political message of the book, is so delicate that, like the silken webs which gleam only for the first fresh hours in the forest, it leaves no trace, but becomes a dream in the memory. And yet this book, which has the freshness of windy rain and the whirling of autumn leaves, is a story of ignominious weakness of the passion that kills, that degrades, that renders life despicable, as Turgenev himself says. *Smoke* is the finest example in literature of a subjective psychological study of passion rendered clearly and objectively in terms of French art. Its character, we will not say its superiority, lies in the extraordinary clearness with which the most obscure mental phenomena are analysed in relation to the ordinary values of daily life. At the precise point of psychological analysis where Tolstoi wanders and does not convince the reader, and at the precise point where Dostoievsky's analysis seems exaggerated and obscure, like a figure looming through the mist, Turgenev throws a ray of light from the outer to the inner world of man, and the two worlds are revealed in the natural depths of their connection. It is in fact difficult to find among the great modern artists men whose natural balance of intellect can be said to equalise their special genius. The Greeks alone present to the world a spectacle of a triumphant harmony in the critical and creative mind of man, and this is their great pre-eminence. But *Smoke* presents the curious feature of a novel (Slav in virtue of its modern

INTRODUCTION

psychological genius) which is classical in its treatment and expression throughout : the balance of Turgenev's intellect reigns ever supreme over the natural morbidity of his subject.

And thus *Smoke* in every sense of the word is a classic for all time.

EDWARD GARNETT.

January 1896.

THE NAMES OF THE CHARACTERS IN THE BOOK

Grigóry [*Grísha*] ... álovitch Litvínov
Tat-yána [*Tánya*] ... róvna Shestóv.
Kapitolína Márkovna.
Rostisláv Bambáev.
Semyón Yákovlevitch Voroshílov.
Stepán Nikoláevitch Gubar-yóv.
Matróna Semyónovna Suhántchikov.
Tit Bindásov.
Pish-tchálkin.
Sozónt Ivánitch Potúgin.
Irína Pávlovna Osínin.
Valerián Vladímirovitch Ratmírov.

In transcribing the Russian names into English—
    a has the sound of *a* in *father*
    e   ,,   ,,   *a* in *pane*.
    i   ,,   ,,   *ce*.
    u ,,   ,,   *oo*.
    y is always consonantal except when it is the last letter of the word.
    g is always hard.

PRESERVATION
REPLACEMENT
REVIEW

I

On the 10th of August 1862, at four o'clock in the afternoon, a great number of people were thronging before the well-known *Konversation* in Baden-Baden. The weather was lovely; everything around—the green trees, the bright houses of the gay city, and the undulating outline of the mountains—everything was in holiday mood, basking in the rays of the kindly sunshine; everything seemed smiling with a sort of blind, confiding delight; and the same glad, vague smile strayed over the human faces too, old and young, ugly and beautiful alike. Even the blackened and whitened visages of the Parisian demi-monde could not destroy the general impression of bright content and elation, while their many-coloured ribbons and feathers and the sparks of gold and steel on their hats and veils involuntarily recalled the intensified brilliance and light fluttering of birds in spring, with their rainbow-tinted wings. But the dry, guttural snapping of the French jargon, heard on all sides could not equal the song of birds, nor be compared with it.

Everything, however, was going on in its accustomed way. The orchestra in the Pavilion played first a medley from the Traviata, then one of Strauss's waltzes, then 'Tell her,' a Russian song, adapted for instruments by an obliging conductor. In the gambling saloons, round the green tables, crowded the same familiar figures, with the same dull, greedy, half-stupefied, half-exasperated, wholly rapacious expression, which the gambling fever lends to all, even the most aristocratic, features. The same well-fed and ultra-fashionably dressed Russian landowner from Tambov with wide staring eyes leaned over the table, and with uncomprehending haste, heedless of the cold smiles of the croupiers themselves, at the very instant of the cry '*rien ne va plus*,' laid with perspiring hand golden rings of *louis d'or* on all the four corners of the roulette, depriving himself by so doing of every possibility of gaining anything, even in case of success. This did not in the least prevent him the same evening from affirming the contrary with disinterested indignation to Prince Kokó, one of the well-known leaders of the aristocratic opposition, the Prince Kokó, who in Paris at the salon of the Princess Mathilde, so happily remarked in the presence of the Emperor: '*Madame, le principe de la propriété est profondément ébranlé en Russie.*' At the Russian tree, *à l'arbre Russe*, our dear fellow-countrymen and countrywomen were assembled after their wont. They approached haughtily and carelessly in fashionable style, greeted each other with dignity and elegant ease, as befits beings who find themselves at the topmost pinnacle of contemporary culture. But when they had met and sat down together, they were absolutely at a loss for anything to say to one another, and had to be content with a pitiful interchange of inanities, or with the exceedingly indecent and exceedingly insipid old jokes of a hopelessly stale French wit, once a journalist, a chattering buffoon with Jewish shoes on his paltry little legs, and a contemptible little beard on his mean little visage. He retailed to them, *à ces princes russes*, all the sweet absurdities from the old comic almanacs *Charivari* and *Tintamarre*, and they, *ces princes russes*, burst into grateful laughter, as though forced in spite of themselves to recognise the crushing superiority of foreign wit, and their own hopeless incapacity to invent anything amusing. Yet here were almost all the '*fine fleur*' of our society, 'all the high-life and mirrors of fashion.' Here was Count X., our incomparable dilettante, a profoundly musical nature, who so divinely recites songs on the piano, but cannot in fact take two notes correctly without fumbling at random on the keys, and sings in a style something between that of a poor gypsy singer and a Parisian hairdresser. Here was our enchanting Baron Q., a master in every line: literature, administration, oratory, and card-sharping. Here, too, was Prince Y., the friend of religion and the people, who in the blissful epoch when the spirit-trade was a monopoly, had made himself betimes a huge fortune by the sale of vodka adulterated with belladonna; and the brilliant General O. O., who had achieved the subjugation of something, and the pacification of something else, and who is nevertheless still a nonenity, and does not know what to do with himself. And R. R. the amusing fat man, who regards himself as a great invalid and a great wit, though he is, in fact, as strong as a bull, and as dull as a post. . . . This R. R. is almost the only man in our day who has preserved the traditions of the dandies of the forties, of the epoch of the 'Hero of our Times,' and the Countess Vorotinsky. He has preserved, too, the special gait with the swing on the heels, and *le culte de la pose* (it cannot even be put into words in Russian), the unnatural deliberation of movement, the sleepy dignity of expression, the immovable, offended-looking countenance, and the habit of interrupting other people's remarks with a yawn, gazing at his own finger-nails, laughing through his nose, suddenly shifting his hat from the back of his head on to his eyebrows, etc. Here, too, were people in government circles, diplomats, big-wigs with European names, men of wisdom and intellect, who imagine that the Golden Bull was an edict of the Pope, and that the English poor-tax is a tax levied on the poor. And here, too, were the hot-blooded, though tongue-tied, devotees of the *dames aux camellias*, young society dandies, with superb partings down the back of their heads, and splendid drooping whiskers, dressed in real London costumes, young bucks whom one would fancy there was nothing to hinder from becoming as vulgar as the illustrious French wit above mentioned. But no! our home products are not in fashion it seems; and Countess S., the celebrated arbitress of fashion and *grand genre*, by spiteful tongues nicknamed 'Queen of the Wasps,' and 'Medusa in a mob-cap,' prefers, in the absence of the French wit, to consort with the Italians, Moldavians, American spiritualists, smart secretaries of foreign embassies, and Germans of effeminate, but prematurely circumspect, physiognomy, of whom the place is full. The example of the Countess is followed by the Princess Babette, she in whose arms Chopin died (the ladies in Europe in whose arms he expired are to be reckoned by thousands); and the Princess Annette, who would have been perfectly captivating, if the simple village washerwoman had not suddenly peeped out in her at times, like a smell of cabbage wafted across the most delicate perfume; and Princess Pachette, to whom the following mischance had occurred: her husband had fallen into a good berth, and all at once, *Dieu sait pourquoi*, he had thrashed the provost and stolen 20,000 roubles of public money; and the laughing Princess Zizi; and the tearful Princess Zozo. They all left their compatriots on one side, and were merciless in their treatment of them. Let us too leave them on one side, these charming ladies, and walk away from the renowned tree near which they sit in such costly but somewhat tasteless costumes, and God grant them relief from the boredom consuming them!

II

A few paces from the 'Russian tree,' at a little table in front of Weber's coffee-house, there was sitting a good-looking man, about thirty, of medium height, thin and dark, with a manly and pleasant face. He sat bending forward with both arms leaning on his stick, with the calm and simple air of a man to whom the idea had not occurred that any one would notice him or pay any attention to him. His large expressive golden-brown eyes were gazing deliberately about him, sometimes screwed up to keep the sunshine out of them, and then watching fixedly some eccentric figure that passed by him while a childlike smile faintly stirred his fine moustache and lips, and his prominent short chin. He wore a roomy coat of German cut, and a soft grey hat hid half of his high forehead. At the first glance he made the impression of an honest, sensible, rather self-confident young man such as there are many in the world. He seemed to be resting from prolonged labours and to be deriving all the more simple-minded amusement from the scene spread out before him because his thoughts were far away, and because they moved too, those thoughts, in a world utterly unlike that which surrounded him at the moment. He was a Russian; his name was Grigory Mihalovitch Litvinov.

We have to make his acquaintance, and so it will be well to relate in a few words his past, which presents little of much interest or complexity.

He was the son of an honest retired official of plebeian extraction, but he was educated, not as one would naturally expect, in the town, but in the country. His mother was of noble family, and had been educated in a government school. She was a good-natured and very enthusiastic creature, not devoid of character, however. Though she was twenty years younger than her husband, she remodelled him, as far as she could, drew him out of the petty official groove into the landowner's way of life, and softened and refined his harsh and stubborn character. Thanks to her, he began to dress with neatness, and to behave with decorum; he came to respect learned men and learning, though, of course, he never took a single book in his hand; he gave up swearing, and tried in every way not to demean himself. He even arrived at walking more quietly and speaking in a subdued voice, mostly of elevated subjects, which cost him no small effort. 'Ah! they ought to be flogged, and that's all about it!' he sometimes thought to himself, but aloud he pronounced: 'Yes, yes, that's so . . . of course; it is a great question.' Litvinov's mother set her household too upon a European footing; she addressed the servants by the plural 'you' instead of the familiar 'thou,' and never allowed any one to gorge himself into a state of lethargy at her table. As regards the property belonging to her, neither she nor her husband was capable of looking after it at all. It had been long allowed to run to waste, but there was plenty of land, with all sorts of useful appurtenances, forest-lands and a lake, on which there had once stood a factory, which had been founded by a zealous but unsystematic owner, and had flourished in the hands of a scoundrelly merchant, and gone utterly to ruin under the superintendence of a conscientious German manager. Madame Litvinov was contented so long as she did not dissipate her fortune or contract debts. Unluckily she could not boast of good health, and she died of consumption in the very year that her son entered the Moscow university. He did not complete his course there owing to circumstances of which the reader will hear more later on, and went back to his provincial home, where he idled away some time without work and without ties, almost without acquaintances. Thanks to the disinclination for active service of the local gentry, who were, however, not so much penetrated by the Western theory of the evils of 'absenteeism,' as by the home-grown conviction that 'one's own shirt is the nearest to one's skin,' he was drawn for military service in 1855, and almost died of typhus in the Crimea, where he spent six months in a mud-hut on the shore of the Putrid Sea, without ever seeing a single ally. After that, he served, not of course without unpleasant experiences, on the councils of the nobility, and after being a little time in the country, acquired a passion for farming. He realised that his mother's property, under the indolent and feeble management of his infirm old father, did not yield a tenth of the revenue it might yield, and that in experienced and skilful hands it might be converted into a perfect gold mine. But he realised, too, that experience and skill were just what he lacked—and he went abroad to study agriculture and technology —to learn them from the first rudiments. More than four years he had spent in Mecklenburg, in Silesia, and in Carlsruhe, and he had travelled in Belgium and in England. He had worked conscientiously and accumulated information;

he had not acquired it easily; but he had persevered through his difficulties to the end, and now with confidence in himself, in his future, and in his usefulness to his neighbours, perhaps even to the whole countryside, he was preparing to return home, where he was summoned with despairing prayers and entreaties in every letter from his father, now completely bewildered by the emancipation, the re-division of lands, and the terms of redemption—by the new régime in short. But why was he in Baden?

Well, he was in Baden because he was from day to day expecting the arrival there of his cousin and betrothed, Tatyana Petrovna Shestov He had known her almost from childhood, and had spent the spring and summer with her at Dresden, where she was living with her aunt. He felt sincere love and profound respect for his young kinswoman, and on the conclusion of his dull preparatory labours, when he was preparing to enter on a new field, to begin real, unofficial duties, he proposed to her as a woman dearly loved, a comrade and a friend, to unite her life with his—for happiness and for sorrow, for labour and for rest, 'for better, for worse' as the English say. She had consented, and he had returned to Carlsruhe, where his books, papers and properties had been left. . . . But why was he at Baden, you ask again?

Well, he was at Baden, because Tatyana's aunt, who had brought her up, Kapitolina Markovna Shestov, an old unmarried lady of fifty-five, a most good-natured, honest, eccentric soul, a free thinker, all aglow with the fire of self-sacrifice and abnegation, an *esprit fort* (she read Strauss, it is true she concealed the fact from her niece) and a democrat, sworn opponent of aristocracy and fashionable society, could not resist the temptation of gazing for once on this aristocratic society in such a fashionable place as Baden. . . . Kapitolina Markovna wore no crinoline and had her white hair cut in a round crop, but luxury and splendour had a secret fascination for her, and it was her favourite pastime to rail at them and express her contempt of them. How could one refuse to gratify the good old lady? But Litvinov was so quiet and simple, he gazed so self-confidently about him, because his life lay so clearly mapped out before him, because his career was defined, and because he was proud of this career, and rejoiced in it as the work of his own hands.

III

'Hullo! hullo! here he is!' he suddenly heard a squeaky voice just above his ear, and a plump hand slapped him on the shoulder. He lifted his head, and perceived one of his few Moscow acquaintances, a certain Bambaev, a good-natured but good-for-nothing fellow. He was no longer young, he had a flabby nose and soft cheeks, that looked as if they had been boiled, dishevelled greasy locks, and a fat squat person. Everlastingly short of cash, and everlastingly in raptures over something, Rostislav Bambaev wandered, aimless but exclamatory, over the face of our long-suffering mother-earth.

'Well, this is something like a meeting!' he repeated, opening wide his sunken eyes, and drawing down his thick lips, over which the straggling dyed moustaches seemed strangely out of place. 'Ah, Baden! All the world runs here like black-beetles! How did you come here, Grisha?'

There was positively no one in the world Bambaev did not address by his Christian name.

'I came here three days ago.'

'From where?'

'Why do you ask?'

'Why indeed? But stop, stop a minute, Grisha. You are, perhaps, not aware who has just arrived here! Gubaryov himself, in person! That's who's here! He came yesterday from Heidelberg. You know him of course?'

'I have heard of him.'

'Is that all? Upon my word! At once, this very minute we will haul you along to him. Not know a man like that! And by the way here's Voroshilov. . . . Stop a minute, Grisha, perhaps you don't know him either? I have the honour to present you to one another. Both learned men! He's a phœnix indeed! Kiss each other!'

And uttering these words, Bambaev turned to a good-looking young man standing near him with a fresh and rosy, but prematurely demure face. Litvinov got up, and, it need hardly be said, did not kiss him, but exchanged a cursory bow with the phœnix, who, to judge from the severity of his demeanour, was not overpleased at this unexpected introduction.

'I said a phœnix, and I will not go back from my word,' continued Bambaev; 'go to

Petersburg, to the military school, and look at the golden board; whose name stands first there? The name of Voroshilov, Semyon Yakovlevitch! But, Gubaryov, Gubaryov, my dear fellow! It's to him we must fly! I absolutely worship that man! And I'm not alone, every one's at his feet! Ah, what a work he is writing, O—O—O! . . .'

'What is his work about?' inquired Litvinov.

'About everything, my dear boy, after the style of Buckle, you know . . . but more profound, more profound. . . . Everything will be solved and made clear in it?'

'And have you read this work yourself?'

'No, I have not read it, and indeed it's a secret, which must not be spread about; but from Gubaryov one may expect everything, everything! Yes!' Bambaev sighed and clasped his hands. 'Ah, if we had two or three intellects like that growing up in Russia, ah, what mightn't we see then, my God! I tell you one thing, Grisha; whatever pursuit you may have been engaged in in these latter days—and I don't even know what your pursuits are in general—whatever your convictions may be—I don't know them either—from him, Gubaryov, you will find something to learn. Unluckily, he is not here for long. We must make the most of him we must go. To him, to him!

A passing dandy with reddish curls and a blue ribbon on his low hat, turned round and stared through his eyeglass with a sarcastic smile at Bambaev. Litvinov felt irritated.

'What are you shouting for?' he said; 'one would think you were hallooing dogs on at a hunt! I have not had dinner yet.'

'Well, think of that! we can go at once to Weber's . . . the three of us . . . capital! You have the cash to pay for me?' he added in an undertone.

'Yes, yes; only, I really don't know——'

'Leave off, please; you will thank me for it, and he will be delighted. Ah, heavens!' Bambaev interrupted himself. 'It's the finale from Ernani they're playing. How delicious!... *A som . . . mo Carlo.* . . . What a fellow I am, though! In tears in a minute. Well, Semyon Yakovlevitch! Voroshilov! shall we go, eh?'

Voroshilov, who had remained all the while standing with immovable propriety, still maintaining his former haughty dignity of demeanour, dropped his eyes expressively, frowned, and muttered something between his teeth... But he did not refuse; and Litvinov thought, 'Well, we may as well do it, as I've plenty of time on my hands.' Bambaev took his arm, but before turning towards the café he beckoned to Isabelle the renowned flower-girl of the Jockey Club : he had conceived the idea of buying a bunch of flowers of her. But the aristocratic flower-girl did not stir; and, indeed, what should induce her to approach a gentleman without gloves, in a soiled fustian jacket, streaky cravat, and boots trodden down at heel, whom she had not even seen in Paris? Then Voroshilov in his turn beckoned to her. To him she responded, and he, taking a tiny bunch of violets from her basket, flung her a florin. He thought to astonish her by his munificence, but not an eyelash on her face quivered, and when he had turned away, she pursed up her mouth contemptuously. Voroshilov was dressed very fashionably, even exquisitely, but the experienced eye of the Parisian girl noted at once in his get-up and in his bearing, in his very walk, which showed traces of premature military drill, the absence of genuine, pure-blooded 'chic.'

When they had taken their seats in the principal dining-hall at Weber's, and ordered dinner, our friends fell into conversation. Bambaev discoursed loudly and hotly upon the immense importance of Gubaryov, but soon he ceased speaking, and, gasping and chewing noisily, drained off glass after glass. Voroshilov eat and drank little, and as it were reluctantly, and after questioning Litvinov as to the nature of his interests, fell to giving expression to his own opinions — not so much on those interests, as on questions of various kinds in general. . . . All at once he warmed up, and set off at a gallop like a spirited horse, boldly and decisively assigning to every syllable, every letter, its due weight, like a confident cadet going up for his 'final' examination, with vehement, but inappropriate gestures. At every instant, since no one interrupted him, he became more eloquent, more emphatic; it seemed as though he were reading a dissertation or lecture. The names of the most recent scientific authorities—with the addition of the dates of the birth or death of each of them—the titles of pamphlets that had only just appeared, and names, names, names . . . fell in showers together from his tongue, affording himself intense satisfaction, reflected in his glowing eyes. Voroshilov, seemingly, despised everything old, and attached value only to the cream of culture, the latest, most advanced points of science; to mention, however inappropriately, a book of some Doctor Zauerbengel on Pennsylvanian prisons, or yesterday's articles in the *Asiatic Journal* on the Vedas and Puranas (he pronounced it *Journal* in the English fashion, though he certainly did not know English) was for him a real joy, a felicity. Litvinov listened and listened to him, and could not make out what could be his special line. At one moment his talk was of the part played by the Celtic race in history; then he was carried away to the ancient world, and discoursed upon the Æginetan marbles, harangued with great warmth on the sculptor living earlier than Phidias, Onetas, who was, however, transformed by him into Jonathan, which lent his whole discourse a half-Biblical, half-American flavour; then he suddenly bounded away to political economy and called Bastiat a fool or a blockhead, 'as bad as Adam Smith and all the physiocrats.' 'Physiocrats,' murmured Bambaev after him ... 'aristocrats?' Among other things Voroshilov called forth an expression of bewilderment on Bambaev's face by a criticism, dropped casually in passing, of Macaulay, as an old-fashioned writer, superseded by modern historical science; as for Gneist, he declared he need scarcely refer to him, and he shrugged his shoulders. Bambaev shrugged his shoulders too. 'And all this at once, without any inducement, before strangers, in a café'—Litvinov reflected, looking at the fair hair, clear eyes, and white teeth of his new acquaintance (he was specially embarrassed by those large sugar-white teeth, and those hands with their inappropriate gesticulations), 'and he doesn't once smile; and with it all, he would seem to be a nice lad, and absolutely inexperienced.' Voroshilov began to calm down at last, his voice, youthfully resonant and shrill as a young cock's, broke a little . . . Bambaev seized the opportunity to declaim verses and again nearly burst into tears, which scandalised one table near them, round which was seated an English family, and set another tittering; two Parisian *cocottes* were dining at this second table with a creature who resembled an ancient baby in a wig. The waiter brought the bill; the friends paid it.

'Well,' cried Bambaev, getting heavily up from his chair, 'now for a cup of coffee, and quick march. There she is, our Russia,' he added, stopping in the doorway, and pointing almost rapturously with his soft red hand to Voroshilov and Litvinov. . . . 'What do you think of her? . . .'

'Russia, indeed,' thought Litvinov; and Voroshilov, whose face had by now regained its concentrated expression, again smiled condescendingly, and gave a little tap with his heels.

Within five minutes they were all three mounting the stairs of the hotel where Stepan Nikolaitch Gubaryov was staying. . . . A tall slender lady, in a hat with a short black veil, was coming quickly down the same staircase.

Catching sight of Litvinov she turned suddenly round to him, and stopped still as though struck by amazement. Her face flushed instantaneously, and then as quickly grew pale under its thick lace veil; but Litvinov did not observe her, and the lady ran down the wide steps more quickly than before.

IV

'GRIGORY LITVINOV, a brick, a true Russian heart. I commend him to you,' cried Bambaev, conducting Litvinov up to a short man of the figure of a country gentleman, with an unbuttoned collar, in a short jacket, grey morning trousers and slippers, standing in the middle of a light, and very well-furnished room; 'and this,' he added, addressing himself to Litvinov, 'is he, the man himself, do you understand? Gubaryov, then, in a word.'

Litvinov stared with curiosity at 'the man himself.' He did not at first sight find in him anything out of the common. He saw before him a gentleman of respectable, somewhat dull exterior, with a broad forehead, large eyes, full lips, a big beard, and a thick neck, with a fixed gaze, bent sidelong and downwards. This gentleman simpered, and said, 'Mmm.... ah ... very pleased, ...' raised his hand to his own face, and at once turning his back on Litvinov, took a few paces upon the carpet, with a slow and peculiar shuffle, as though he were trying to slink along unseen. Gubaryov had the habit of continually walking up and down, and constantly plucking and combing his beard with the tips of his long hard nails. Besides Gubaryov, there was also in the room a lady of about fifty, in a shabby silk dress, with an excessively mobile face almost as yellow as a lemon, a little black moustache on her upper lip, and eyes which moved so quickly that they seemed as though they were jumping out of her head; there was too a broad-shouldered man sitting bent up in a corner.

'Well, honoured Matrona Semyonovna,' began Gubaryov, turning to the lady, and apparently not considering it necessary to introduce Litvinov to her, 'what was it you were beginning to tell us?'

The lady (her name was Matrona Semyonovna Suhantchikov—she was a widow, childless, and not rich, and had been travelling from country to country for two years past) began with peculiar exasperated vehemence:

'Well, so he appears before the prince and says to him: "Your Excellency," he says, "in such an office and such a position as yours, what will it cost you to alleviate my lot? You," he says, "cannot but respect the purity of my ideas! And is it possible," he says, "in these days to persecute a man for his ideas?" And what do you suppose the prince did, that cultivated dignitary in that exalted position?'"

'Why, what did he do?' observed Gubaryov, lighting a cigarette with a meditative air.

The lady drew herself up and held out her bony right hand, with the first finger separated from the rest.

'He called his groom and said to him, "Take off that man's coat at once, and keep it yourself. I make you a present of that coat!"'

'And did the groom take it?' asked Bambaev, throwing up his arms.

'He took it and kept it. And that was done by Prince Barnaulov, the well-known rich grandee, invested with special powers, the representative of the government. What is one to expect after that!'

The whole frail person of Madame Suhantchikov was shaking with indignation, spasms passed over her face, her withered bosom was heaving convulsively under her flat corset; of her eyes it is needless to speak, they were fairly leaping out of her head. But then they were always leaping, whatever she might be talking about.

'A crying shame, a crying shame!' cried Bambaev. 'No punishment could be bad enough!'

'Mmm. . . . Mmm. . . . From top to bottom it's all rotten,' observed Gubaryov, without raising his voice, however. In that case punishment is not . . . that needs . . . other measures.'

'But is it really true?' commented Litvinov.

'Is it true?' broke in Madame Suhantchikov. 'Why, that one can't even dream of doubting . . . can't even d—d—d—ream of it.' She pronounced these words with such energy that she was fairly shaking with the effort. 'I was told of that by a very trustworthy man. And you, Stepan Nikolaitch, know him — Elistratov, Kapiton. He heard it himself from eyewitnesses, spectators of this disgraceful scene.'

'What Elistratov?' inquired Gubaryov. 'The one who was in Kazan?'

'Yes. I know, Stepan Nikolaitch, a rumour was spread about him that he took bribes there from some contractors or distillers. But then who is it says so? Pelikanov! And how can one believe Pelikanov, when every one knows he is simply—a spy!'

'No, with your permission, Matrona Semyonovna,' interposed Bambaev, 'I am friends with Pelikanov, he is not a spy at all.'

'Yes, yes, that's just what he is, a spy!'

'But wait a minute, kindly——'

'A spy, a spy!' shrieked Madame Suhantchikov.

'No, no, one minute, I tell you what,' shrieked Bambaev in his turn.

'A spy, a spy,' persisted Madame Suhantchikov.

'No, no! There's Tentelyev now, that's a different matter,' roared Bambaev with all the force of his lungs.

Madame Suhantchikov was silent for a moment.

'I know for a fact about that gentleman,' he continued in his ordinary voice, 'that when he was summoned before the secret police, he grovelled at the feet of the Countess Blazenkrampff and kept whining, "Save me, intercede for me!" But Pelikanov never demeaned himself to baseness like that.'

'Mm. . . . Tentelyev . . .' muttered Gubaryov, 'that . . . that ought to be noted.'

Madame Suhantchikov shrugged her shoulders contemptuously.

'They're one worse than another,' she said, 'but I know a still better story about Tentelyev. He was, as every one knows, a most horrible despot with his serfs, though he gave himself out for an emancipator. Well, he was once at some friend's house in Paris, and suddenly in comes Madame Beecher Stowe—you know, *Uncle Tom's Cabin*. Tentelyev, who's an awfully pushing fellow, began asking the host to present him; but directly she heard his name. "What?"

she said, "he presumes to be introduced to the author of *Uncle Tom*?" And she gave him a slap on the cheek! "Go away!" she says, "at once!" And what do you think? Tentelyev took his hat and slunk away, pretty crestfallen.'

'Come, I think that's exaggerated,' observed Bambaev. '"Go away" she certainly did say, that's a fact, but she didn't give him a smack!'

'She did, she did!' repeated Madam Suhantchikov with convulsive intensity: 'I am not talking idle gossip. And you are friends with men like that!'

'Excuse me, excuse me, Matrona Semyonovna, I never spoke of Tentelyev as a friend of mine; I was speaking of Pelikanov.'

'Well, if it's not Tentelyev, its another. Mihnyov, for example.'

'What did he do then?' asked Bambaev, already showing signs of alarm.

'What? Is it possible you don't know? He exclaimed on the Poznesensky Prospect in the hearing of all the world that all the liberals ought to be in prison; and what's more, an old schoolfellow came to him, a poor man of course, and said, "Can I come to dinner with you?" And this was his answer. "No, impossible; I have two counts dining with me to-day . . . get along with you!"'

'But that's slander, upon my word!' vociferated Bambaev.

'Slander? . . . slander? In the first place, Prince Vahrushkin, who was also dining at your Mihnyov's——'

'Prince Vahrushkin,' Gubaryov interpolated severely, 'is my cousin; but I don't allow him to enter my house. . . . So there is no need to mention him even.'

'In the second place,' continued Madame Suhantchikov, with a submissive nod in Gubaryov's direction, 'Praskovya Yakovlevna told me so herself.'

'You have hit on a fine authority to quote! Why, she and Sarkizov are the greatest scandal-mongers going.'

'I beg your pardon, Sarkizov is a liar, certainly. He filched the very pall of brocade off his dead father's coffin. I will never dispute that; but Praskovya Yakovlovna—there's no comparison! Remember how magnanimously she parted from her husband! But you, I know, are always ready——'

'Come, enough, enough, Matrona Semyonovna,' said Bambaev, interrupting her, 'let us give up this tittle-tattle, and take a loftier flight. I am not new to the work, you know. Have you read *Mlle. de la Quintinie*? That's something charming now! And quite in accord with your principles at the same time!'

'I never read novels now,' was Madame Suhantchikov's dry and sharp reply.

'Why?'

'Because I have not the time now; I have no thoughts now but for one thing, sewing machines.'

'What machines?' inquired Litvinov.

'Sewing, sewing; all women ought to provide themselves with sewing-machines, and form societies; in that way they will all be enabled to earn their living, and will become independent at once. In no other way can they ever be emancipated. That is an important, most important social question. I had such an argument about it with Boleslav Stadnitsky. Boleslav Stadnitsky is a marvellous nature, but he looks at these things in an awfully frivolous spirit. He does nothing but laugh. Idiot!'

'All will in their due time be called to account, from all it will be exacted,' pronounced Gubaryov deliberately, in a tone half-professorial, half-prophetic.

'Yes, yes,' repeated Bambaev, 'it will be exacted, precisely so, it will be exacted. But, Stepan Nikolaitch,' he added, dropping his voice, 'how goes the great work?'

'I am collecting materials,' replied Gubaryov,

knitting his brows; and, turning to Litvinov, whose head began to swim from the medley of unfamiliar names, and the frenzy of backbiting, he asked him what subjects he was interested in.

Litvinov satisfied his curiosity.

'Ah! to be sure, the natural sciences. That is useful, as training; as training, not as an end in itself. The end at present should be . . . mm. . . . should be . . . different. Allow me to ask what views do you hold?'

'What views?'

'Yes, that is, more accurately speaking, what are your political views?'

Litvinov smiled.

'Strictly speaking, I have no political views.'

The broad-shouldered man sitting in the corner raised his head quickly at these words and looked attentively at Litvinov.

'How is that?' observed Gubaryov with peculiar gentleness. 'Have you not yet reflected on the subject, or have you grown weary of it?'

'How shall I say? It seems to me that for us Russians, it is too early yet to have political views or to imagine that we have them. Observe that I attribute to the word "political" the meaning which belongs to it by right, and that——'

'Aha! he belongs to the undeveloped,' Gubaryov interrupted him, with the same gentleness, and going up to Voroshilov, he asked him: ' Had he read the pamphlet he had given him?'

Voroshilov, to Litvinov's astonishment, had not uttered a word ever since his entrance, but had only knitted his brows and rolled his eyes (as a rule he was either speechifying or else perfectly dumb). He now expanded his chest in soldierly fashion, and with a tap of his heels, nodded assent.

'Well, and how was it? Did you like it?'

'As regards the fundamental principles, I liked it; but I did not agree with the inferences.'

'Mmm.... Andrei Ivanitch praised that pamphlet, however. You must expand your doubts to me later.'

'You desire it in writing?'

Gubaryov was obviously surprised; he had not expected this; however, after a moment's thought, he replied:

'Yes, in writing. By the way, I will ask you to explain to me your views also .. in regard to ... in regard to associations.'

'Associations on Lassalle's system, do you desire, or on the system of Schulze-Delitzsch?'

'Mmm.... on both. For us Russians, you understand, the financial aspect of the matter is specially important. Yes, and the *artel* . . . as the germ. . . . All that, one must take note of. One must go deeply into it. And the question, too, of the land to be apportioned to the peasants. . . .'

'And you, Stepan Nikolaitch, what is your view as to the number of acres suitable?' inquired Voroshilov, with reverential delicacy in his voice.

'Mmm. . . . and the commune?' articulated Gubaryov, deep in thought, and biting a tuft of his beard he stared at the table-leg. 'The commune! . . . Do you understand. That is a grand word! Then what is the significance of these conflagrations? these . . . these government measures against Sunday-schools, reading-rooms, journals? And the refusal of the peasants to sign the charters regulating their position in the future? And finally, what of what is happening in Poland? Don't you see that . . . mmm. . . . that we . . we have to unite with the people . . . find out . . . find out their views——' Suddenly a heavy, almost a wrathful emotion seemed to take possession of Gubaryov; he even grew black in the face and breathed heavily, but still did not raise his eyes, and continued to gnaw at his beard. 'Can't you see——'

'Yevseyev is a wretch!' Madame Suhantchikov burst out noisily all of a sudden. Bambaev had been relating something to her in a voice lowered out of respect for their host. Gubaryov turned round swiftly on his heels, and again began limping about the room.

Fresh guests began to arrive; towards the end of the evening a good many people were assembled. Among them came, too, Mr. Yevseyev whom Madame Suhantchikov had vilified so cruelly. She entered into conversation with him very cordially, and asked him to escort her home; there arrived too a certain Pishtchalkin, an ideal mediator, one of those men of precisely whom perhaps Russia stands in need—a man, that is, narrow, of little information, and no great gifts, but conscientious, patient, and honest; the peasants of his district almost worshipped him, and he regarded himself very respectfully as a creature genuinely deserving of esteem. A few officers, too, were there, escaped for a brief furlough to Europe, and rejoicing—though of course warily, and ever mindful of their colonel in the background of their brains—in the opportunity of dallying a little with intellectual—even rather dangerous—people; two lanky students from Heidelberg came hurrying in, one looked about him very contemptuously, the other giggled spasmodically . . . both were very ill at ease;

after them a Frenchman—a so-called *petit jeune homme*—poked his nose in; a nasty, silly, pitiful little creature, . . . who enjoyed some repute among his fellow *commis-voyageurs* on the theory that Russian countesses had fallen in love with him; for his own part, his reflections were centred more upon getting a supper gratis; the last to appear was Tit Bindasov, in appearance a rollicking German student, in reality a skinflint, in words a terrorist, by vocation a police-officer, a friend of Russian merchants' wives and Parisian *cocottes*; bald, toothless, and drunken; he arrived very red and sodden, affirming that he had lost his last farthing to that blackguard Benazet; in reality, he had won sixteen guldens. . . . In short, there were a number of people. Remarkable—really remarkable—was the respect with which all these people treated Gubaryov as a preceptor or chief; they laid their ideas before him, and submitted them to his judgment; and he replied by muttering, plucking at his beard, averting his eyes, or by some disconnected, meaningless words, which were at once seized upon as the utterances of the loftiest wisdom Gubaryov himself seldom interposed in the discussions; but the others strained their lungs to the utmost to make up for it. It happened more than once that three or four were shouting for ten minutes together, and all were content and understood. The conversation lasted till after midnight, and was as usual distinguished by the number and variety of the subjects discussed. Madame Suhantchikov talked about Garibaldi, about a certain Karl Ivanovitch, who had been flogged by the serfs of his own household, about Napoleon III., about women's work, about a merchant, Pleskatchov, who had designedly caused the death of twelve workwomen, and had received a medal for it with the inscription 'for public services'; about the proletariat, about the Georgian Prince Tchuktcheulidzov, who had shot his wife with a cannon, and about the future of Russia. Pishtchalkin, too, talked of the future of Russia, and of the spirit monopoly, and of the significance of nationalities, and of how he hated above everything what was vulgar. There was an outburst all of a sudden from Voroshilov; in a single breath, almost choking himself, he mentioned Draper, Virchow, Shelgunov, Bichat, Helmholtz, Star, St. Raymund, Johann Müller the physiologist, and Johann Müller the historian —obviously confounding them—Taine, Renan, Shtchapov; and then Thomas Nash, Peele, Greene. . . . 'What sort of queer fish may they be?' Bambaev muttered bewildered, Shakespeare's predecessors having the same relation

to him as the ranges of the Alps to Mont Blanc.
Voroshilov replied cuttingly, and he too touched
on the future of Russia. Bambaev also spoke
of the future of Russia, and even depicted it in
glowing colours: but he was thrown into special
raptures over the thought of Russian music, in
which he saw something. 'Ah! great indeed!'
and in confirmation he began humming a song
of Varlamov's, but was soon interrupted by a
general shout, ' He is singing the *Miserere* from
the *Trovatore*, and singing it excruciatingly too.'
One little officer was reviling Russian literature
in the midst of the hubbub; another was quoting verses from *Sparks*; but Tit Bindasov
went even further; he declared that all these
swindlers ought to have their teeth knocked
out, . . . and that's all about it, but he did not
particularise who were the swindlers alluded to.
The smoke from the cigars became stifling; all
were hot and exhausted, every one was hoarse,
all eyes were growing dim, and the perspiration
stood out in drops on every face. Bottles of
iced beer were brought in and drunk off instantaneously. 'What was I saying?' remarked
one; 'and with whom was I disputing, and
about what?' inquired another. And among
all the uproar and the smoke, Gubaryov walked
indefatigably up and down as before, swaying
from side to side and twitching at his beard;

now listening, turning an ear to some controversy, now putting in a word of his own; and every one was forced to feel that he, Gubaryov, was the source of it all, that he was the master here, and the most eminent personality. . . .

Litvinov, towards ten o'clock, began to have a terrible headache, and, taking advantage of a louder outburst of general excitement, went off quietly unobserved. Madame Suhantchikov had recollected a fresh act of injustice of Prince Barnaulov; he had all but given orders to have some one's ears bitten off.

The fresh night air enfolded Litvinov's flushed face caressingly, the fragrant breeze breathed on his parched lips. 'What is it,' he thought as he went along the dark avenue, 'that I have been present at? Why were they met together? What were they shouting, scolding, and making such a pother about? What was it all for?' Litvinov shrugged his shoulders, and turning into Weber's, he picked up a newspaper and asked for an ice. The newspaper was taken up with a discussion on the Roman question, and the ice turned out to be very nasty. He was already preparing to go home, when suddenly an unknown person in a wide-brimmed hat drew near, and saying in Russian: 'I hope I am not in your way?' sat down at his table. Only then, after a closer glance at the stranger, Litvinov recognised him as the broad-shouldered gentleman hidden away in a corner at Gubaryov's, who had stared at him with such attention when the conversation had turned on political views. During the whole evening this gentleman had not once opened his mouth, and now, sitting down near Litvinov, and taking off his hat, he looked at him with an expression of friendliness and some embarrassment.

V

'Mr. Gubaryov, at whose rooms I had the pleasure of meeting you to-day,' he began, 'did not introduce me to you; so that, with your leave, I will now introduce myself—Potugin, retired councillor. I was in the department of finances in St. Petersburg. I hope you do not think it strange. . . . I am not in the habit as a rule of making friends so abruptly . . . but with you. . . .'

Here Potugin grew rather mixed, and he asked the waiter to bring him a little glass of kirsch-wasser. 'To give me courage,' he added with a smile.

Litvinov looked with redoubled interest at the last of all the new persons with whom it had been his lot to be brought into contact that day. His thought was at once, 'He is not the same as those.'

Certainly he was not. There sat before him, drumming with delicate fingers on the edge of the table, a broad-shouldered man, with an ample frame on short legs, a downcast head of curly hair, with very intelligent and very mournful eyes under bushy brows, a thick well-cut mouth, bad teeth, and that purely Russian nose to which is assigned the epithet 'potato'; a man of awkward, even odd exterior; at least, he was certainly not of a common type. He was carelessly dressed; his old-fashioned coat hung on him like a sack, and his cravat was twisted awry. His sudden friendliness, far from striking Litvinov as intrusive, secretly flattered him; it was impossible not to see that it was not a common practice with this man to attach himself to strangers. He made a curious impression on Litvinov; he awakened in him respect and liking, and a kind of involuntary compassion.

'I am not in your way then?' he repeated in a soft, rather languid and faint voice, which was marvellously in keeping with his whole personality.

'No, indeed,' replied Litvinov; 'quite the contrary, I am very glad.'

'Really? Well, then, I am glad too. I have heard a great deal about you; I know what you are engaged in, and what your plans are. It's a good work. That's why you were silent this evening.'

'Yes; you too said very little, I fancy,' observed Litvinov.

Potugin sighed. 'The others said enough and to spare. I listened. Well,' he added, after a moment's pause, raising his eyebrows with a rather humorous expression, 'did you like our building of the Tower of Babel?'

'That's just what it was. You have expressed it capitally. I kept wanting to ask those gentlemen what they were in such a fuss about.'

Potugin sighed again.

'That's the whole point of it, that they don't know that themselves. In former days the expression used about them would have been: "they are the blind instruments of higher ends"; well, nowadays we make use of sharper epithets. And take note that I am not in the least intending to blame them; I will say more, they are all . . . that is, almost all, excellent people. Of Madame Suhantchikov, for instance, I know for certain much that is good; she gave away the last of her fortune to two poor nieces. Even admitting that the desire of doing something picturesque, of showing herself off, was not without its influence on her, still you will agree that it was a remarkable act of self-sacrifice in a woman not herself well-off! Of Mr. Pishtchalkin there is no need to speak even; the peasants of his district will certainly in time present him with a silver bowl like a pumpkin, and perhaps even a holy picture representing his patron saint, and though he will tell them in his speech of thanks that he does not deserve such an honour, he won't tell the truth there; he does deserve it. Mr. Bambaev, your friend, has a wonderfully good heart; it's true that it's with him as with the poet Yazikov, who they say used to sing the praises of Bacchic revelry, sitting over a book and sipping water; his enthusiasm is completely without a special object, still it is enthusiasm; and Mr. Voroshilov, too, is the most good-natured fellow; like all his sort, all men who've taken the first prizes at school, he's an *aide-de-camp* of the sciences, and he even holds his tongue sententiously, but then he is so young. Yes, yes, they are all excellent people, and when you come to results, there's nothing to show for it; the ingredients are all first-rate, but the dish is not worth eating.'

Litvinov listened to Potugin with growing astonishment: every phrase, every turn of his slow but self-confident speech betrayed both the power of speaking and the desire to speak.

Potugin did, in fact, like speaking, and could speak well; but, as a man in whom life had succeeded in wearing away vanity, he waited with philosophic calm for a good opportunity, a meeting with a kindred spirit.

'Yes, yes,' he began again, with the special dejected but not peevish humour peculiar to him, ' it is all very strange. And there is something else I want you to note. Let a dozen Englishmen, for example, come together, and they will at once begin to talk of the submarine telegraph, or the tax on paper, or a method of tanning rats' skins,—of something, that's to say, practical and definite; a dozen Germans, and of course Schleswig-Holstein and the unity of Germany will be brought on the scene; given a dozen Frenchmen, and the conversation will infallibly turn upon amorous adventures, however much you try to divert them from the subject; but let a dozen Russians meet together, and instantly there springs up the question—you had an opportunity of being convinced of the fact this evening—the question of the significance and the future of Russia, and in terms so general, beginning with creation, without facts or conclusions. They worry and worry away at that unlucky subject, as children chew away at a bit of india-rubber—neither for pleasure nor profit, as the saying is. Well, then, of course the rotten West comes in for its share. It's a curious thing, it beats us at every point, this West—but yet we declare that it's rotten! And if only we had a genuine contempt for it,' pursued Potugin, 'but that's really all cant and humbug. We can do well enough as far as abuse goes, but the opinion of the West is the only thing we value, the opinion, that's to say, of the Parisian loafers. . . . I know a man—a good fellow, I fancy—the father of a family, and no longer young; he was thrown into deep dejection for some days because in a Parisian restaurant he had asked for *une portion de biftek aux pommes de terre*, and a real Frenchman thereupon shouted: *Garçon! biftek pommes!* My friend was ready to die with shame, and after that he shouted everywhere, *Biftek pommes!* and taught others to do the same. The very *cocottes* are surprised at the reverential trepidation with which our young barbarians enter their shameful drawing-rooms. "Good God!" they are thinking, "is this really where I am, with no less a person than Anna Deslions herself!"'

'Tell me, pray,' continued Litvinov, 'to what do you ascribe the influence Gubaryov undoubtedly has over all about him? Is it his talent, his abilities?'

'No, no; there is nothing of that sort about him. . . .'

'His personal character is it, then?'

'Not that either, but he has a strong will. We Slavs, for the most part, as we all know, are badly off for that commodity, and we grovel before it. It is Mr. Gubaryov's will to be a ruler, and every one has recognised him as a ruler. What would you have? The government has freed us from the dependence of serfdom —and many thanks to it! but the habits of slavery are too deeply ingrained in us; we cannot easily be rid of them. We want a master in everything and everywhere; as a rule this master is a living person, sometimes it is some so-called tendency which gains authority over us. . . . At present, for instance, we are all the bondslaves of natural science. . . . Why, owing to what causes, we take this bondage upon us, that is a matter difficult to see into; but such seemingly is our nature. But the great thing is, that we should have a master. Well, here he is amongst us; that means he is ours, and we can afford to despise everything else! Simply slaves! And our pride is slavish, and slavish too is our humility. If a new master arises— it's all over with the old one. Then it was Yakov, and now it is Sidor; we box Yakov's ears and kneel to Sidor! Call to mind how many tricks of that sort have been played amongst us! We talk of scepticism as our special characteristic; but even in our scepticism we are not like a free man fighting with a sword, but like a lackey hitting out with his fist, and very likely he is doing even that at his master's bidding. Then, we are a soft people too ; it's not difficult to keep the curb on us. So that's the way Mr. Gubaryov has become a power among us; he has chipped and chipped away at one point, till he has chipped himself into success. People see that he is a man who has a great opinion of himself, who believes in himself, and commands. That's the great thing, that he can command; it follows that he must be right, and we ought to obey him. All our sects, our Onuphrists and Akulinists, were founded exactly in that way. He who holds the rod is the corporal.'

Potugin's cheeks were flushed and his eyes grew dim ; but, strange to say, his speech, cruel and even malicious as it was, had no touch of bitterness, but rather of sorrow, genuine and sincere sorrow.

'How did you come to know Gubaryov?' asked Litvinov.

'I have known him a long while. And observe, another peculiarity among us ; a certain writer, for example, spent his whole life in inveighing in prose and verse against drunkenness, and attacking the system of the drink monopoly, and lo and behold ! he went and bought two spirit distilleries and opened a hundred drink-shops—and it made no difference !

Any other man might have been wiped off the face of the earth, but he was not even reproached for it. And here is Mr. Gubaryov; he is a Slavophil and a democrat and a socialist and anything you like, but his property has been and is still managed by his brother, a master of the old style, one of those who were famous for their fists. And the very Madame Suhantchikov, who makes Mrs. Beecher Stowe box Tentelyev's ears, is positively in the dust before Gubaryov's feet. And you know the only thing he has to back him is that he reads clever books, and always gets at the pith of them. You could see for yourself to-day what sort of gift he has for expression; and thank God, too, that he does talk little, and keeps in his shell. For when he is in good spirits, and lets himself go, then it's more than even I, patient as I am, can stand. He begins by coarse joking and telling filthy anecdotes . . . yes, really, our majestic Mr. Gubaryov tells filthy anecdotes, and guffaws so revoltingly over them all the time.'

'Are you so patient?' observed Litvinov. 'I should have supposed the contrary. But let me ask your name and your father's name?'

Potugin sipped a little kirsch-wasser.

'My name is Sozont. . . . Sozont Ivanitch. They gave me that magnificent name in honour of a kinsman, an archimandrite, to whom I am indebted for nothing else. I am, if I may venture so to express myself, of most reverend stock. And as for your doubts about my patience, they are quite groundless: I am very patient. I served for twenty-two years under the authority of my own uncle, an actual councillor of state, Irinarh Potugin. You don't know him?'

'No.'

'I congratulate you. No, I am patient. "But let us return to our first head," as my esteemed colleague, who was burned alive some centuries ago, the protopope Avvakum, used to say. I am amazed, my dear sir, at my fellow-countrymen. They are all depressed, they all walk with downcast heads, and at the same time they are all filled with hope, and on the smallest excuse they lose their heads and fly off into ecstasies. Look at the Slavophils even, among whom Mr. Gubaryov reckons himself: they are most excellent people, but there is the same mixture of despair and exultation, they too live in the future tense. Everything will be, will be, if you please. In reality there is nothing done, and Russia for ten whole centuries has created nothing of its own, either in government, in law, in science, in art, or even in handicraft. . . . But wait a little, have patience; it is all coming. And why is it coming; give us leave to inquire? Why because we, to be sure, the cultured classes are all worthless; but the people ... Oh, the great people! You see that peasant's smock? That is the source that everything is to come from. All the other idols have broken down; let us have faith in the smock-frock. Well, but suppose the smock-frock fails us? No, it will not fail. Read Kohanovsky, and cast your eyes up to heaven! Really, if I were a painter, I would paint a picture of this sort: a cultivated man standing before a peasant, doing him homage: heal me, dear master-peasant, I am perishing of disease; and a peasant doing homage in his turn to the cultivated man: teach me, dear master-gentleman, I am perishing from ignorance. Well, and of course, both are standing still. But what we ought to do is to feel really humble for a little—not only in words—and to borrow from our elder brothers what they have invented already before us and better than us! Waiter, *noch ein Gläschen Kirsch*! You mustn't think I'm a drunkard, but alcohol loosens my tongue.'

'After what you have just said,' observed Litvinov with a smile, 'I need not even inquire to which party you belong, and what is your opinion about Europe. But let me make one observation to you. You say that we ought to borrow from our elder brothers: but how can we borrow without consideration of the conditions of climate and of soil, the local and national peculiarities? My father, I recollect, ordered from Butenop a cast-iron thrashing machine highly recommended; the machine was very good, certainly—but what happened? For five long years it remained useless in the barn, till it was replaced by a wooden American one—far more suitable to our ways and habits, as the American machines are as a rule. One cannot borrow at random, Sozont Ivanitch.'

Potugin lifted his head.

'I did not expect such a criticism as that from you, excellent Grigory Mihalovitch,' he began, after a moment's pause. 'Who wants to make you borrow at random? Of course you steal what belongs to another man, not because it is some one else's, but because it suits you; so it follows that you consider, you make a selection. And as for results, pray don't let us be unjust to ourselves; there will be originality enough in them by virtue of those very local, climatic, and other conditions which you mention. Only lay good food before it, and the natural stomach will digest it in its own way; and in time, as the organism gains in vigour, it will give it a sauce of its own. Take our language even as an instance. Peter the Great deluged it with thousands of foreign words, Dutch, French, and

German; those words expressed ideas with which the Russian people had to be familiarised; without scruple or ceremony Peter poured them wholesale by bucketsful into us. At first, of course, the result was something of a monstrous product; but later there began precisely that process of digestion to which I have alluded. The ideas had been introduced and assimilated; the foreign forms evaporated gradually, and the language found substitutes for them from within itself; and now your humble servant, the most mediocre stylist, will undertake to translate any page you like out of Hegel—yes, indeed, out of Hegel—without making use of a single word not Slavonic. What has happened with the language, one must hope will happen in other departments. It all turns on the question: is it a nature of strong vitality? and our nature—well, it will stand the test; it has gone through greater trials than that. Only nations in a state of nervous debility, feeble nations, need fear for their health and their independence, just as it is only weak-minded people who are capable of falling into triumphant rhapsodies over the fact that we are Russians. I am very careful over my health, but I don't go into ecstasies over it: I should be ashamed.'

'That is all very true, Sozont Ivanitch,' observed Litvinov in his turn; 'but why inevitably expose ourselves to such tests? You say yourself that at first the result was monstrous! Well, what if that monstrous product had persisted? Indeed it has persisted, as you know yourself.'

'Only not in the language—and that means a great deal! And it is our people, not I, who have done it; I am not to blame because they are destined to go through a discipline of this kind. "The Germans have developed in a normal way," cry the Slavophils, "let us too have a normal development!" But how are you to get it when the very first historical step taken by our race—the summoning of a prince from over the sea to rule over them—is an irregularity, an abnormality, which is repeated in every one of us down to the present day; each of us, at least once in his life, has certainly said to something foreign, not Russian: "Come, rule and reign over me!" I am ready, of course, to agree that when we put a foreign substance into our own body we cannot tell for certain what it is we are putting there, bread or poison; yet it is a well-known thing that you can never get from bad to good through what is better, but always through a worse state of transition, and poison too is useful in medicine. It is only fit for fools or knaves to point with triumph to the poverty of the peasants after the emancipation, and the increase of drunkenness since the abolition of the farming of the spirit-tax. . . . Through worse to better!'

Potugin passed his hand over his face. 'You asked me what was my opinion of Europe,' he began again: 'I admire her, and am devoted to her principles to the last degree, and don't in the least think it necessary to conceal the fact. I have long—no, not long—for some time ceased to be afraid to give full expression to my convictions—and I saw that you too had no hesitation in informing Mr. Gubaryov of your own way of thinking. Thank God I have given up paying attention to the ideas and points of view and habits of the man I am conversing with. Really, I know of nothing worse than that quite superfluous cowardice, that cringing desire to be agreeable, by virtue of which you may see an important dignitary among us trying to ingratiate himself with some little student who is quite insignificant in his eyes, positively playing down to him, with all sorts of tricks and devices. Even if we admit that the dignitary may do it out of desire for popularity, what induces us common folk to shuffle and degrade ourselves. Yes, yes, I am a Westerner, I am devoted to Europe: that's to say, speaking more accurately, I am devoted to culture—the culture at which they make fun so wittily among us just now—and to civilisation—yes, yes, that is a better word—and I love it with my whole heart and believe in it, and I have no other belief, and never shall have. That word, ci-vi-li-sa-tion (Potugin pronounced each syllable with full stress and emphasis), is intelligible, and pure, and holy, and all the other ideals, nationality, glory, or what you like—they smell of blood. . . . Away with them!'

'Well, but Russia, Sozont Ivanitch, your country—you love it?'

Potugin passed his hand over his face. 'I love her passionately and passionately hate her.'

Litvinov shrugged his shoulders.

'That's stale, Sozont Ivanitch, that's a commonplace.'

'And what of it? So that's what you're afraid of! A commonplace! I know many excellent commonplaces. Here, for example, Law and Liberty is a well-known commonplace. Why, do you consider it's better as it is with us, lawlessness and bureaucratic tyranny? And, besides, all those phrases by which so many young heads are turned: vile bourgeoisie, *souveraineté du peuple*, right to labour, aren't they commonplaces too? And as for love, inseparable from hate . . .'

'Byronism,' interposed Litvinov, 'the romanticism of the thirties.'

'Excuse me, you're mistaken; such a mingling of emotions was first mentioned by Catullus, the Roman poet Catullus,[1] two thousand years ago. I have read that, for I know a little Latin, thanks to my clerical origin, if so I may venture to express myself. Yes, indeed, I both love and hate my Russia, my strange, sweet, nasty, precious country. I have left her just now. I want a little fresh air after sitting for twenty years on a clerk's high stool in a government office; I have left Russia, and I am happy and contented here; but I shall soon go back again: I feel that. It's a beautiful land of gardens—but our wild berries will not grow here.'

'You are happy and contented, and I too like the place,' said Litvinov, 'and I came here to study; but that does not prevent me from seeing things like that.'

He pointed to two *cocottes* who passed by, attended by a little group of members of the Jockey Club, grimacing and lisping, and to the gambling saloon, full to overflowing in spite of the lateness of the hour.

'And who told you I am blind to that?' Potugin broke in. 'But pardon my saying it, your remark reminds me of the triumphant

[1] Odi et amo. Quare id faciam, fortasse requiris.
Nescio: sed fieri sentio, et excrucior.—CATULL. lxxxvi.

allusions made by our unhappy journalists at the time of the Crimean war, to the defects in the English War Department, exposed in the *Times*. I am not an optimist myself, and all humanity, all our life, all this comedy with tragic issues presents itself to me in no roseate colours: but why fasten upon the West what is perhaps ingrained in our very human nature? That gambling hall is disgusting, certainly; but is our home-bred card-sharping any lovelier, think you? No, my dear Grigory Mihalovitch, let us be more humble, more retiring. A good pupil sees his master's faults, but he keeps a respectful silence about them; these very faults are of use to him, and set him on the right path. But if nothing will satisfy you but sharpening your teeth on the unlucky West, there goes Prince Kokó at a gallop, he will most likely lose in a quarter of an hour over the green table the hardly earned rent wrung from a hundred and fifty families; his nerves are upset, for I saw him at Marx's to-day turning over a pamphlet of Vaillot. . . . He will be a capital person for you to talk to!'

'But, please, please,' said Litvinov hurriedly, seeing that Potugin was getting up from his place, 'I know Prince Kokó very little, and besides, of course, I greatly prefer talking to you.'

'Thanks very much,' Potugin interrupted

him, getting up and making a bow; 'but I have already had a good deal of conversation with you; that's to say, really, I have talked alone, and you have probably noticed yourself that a man is always as it were ashamed and awkward when he has done all the talking, especially so on a first meeting, as if to show what a fine fellow one is. Good-bye for the present. And I repeat I am very glad to have made your acquaintance.'

'But wait a minute, Sozont Ivanitch, tell me at least where you live, and whether you intend to remain here long.'

Potugin seemed a little put out.

'I shall remain about a week in Baden. We can meet here though, at Weber's or at Marx's, or else I will come to you.'

'Still I must know your address.'

'Yes. But you see I am not alone.'

'You are married?' asked Litvinov suddenly.

'No, good heavens!... what an absurd idea! But I have a girl with me.'...

'Oh!' articulated Litvinov, with a face of studied politeness, as though he would ask pardon, and he dropped his eyes.

'She is only six years old,' pursued Potugin. 'She's an orphan... the daughter of a lady... a good friend of mine. So we had better meet here. Good-bye.'

flowers. Again something stirred in Litvinov's memory. He asked the man what the lady looked like, and the servant informed him that she was tall and grandly dressed and had a veil over her face. 'A Russian countess most likely,' he added.

'What makes you think that?' asked Litvinov.

'She gave me two guldens,' responded the servant with a grin.

Litvinov dismissed him, and for a long while after he stood in deep thought before the window; at last, however, with a wave of his hand, he began again upon the letter from the country. His father poured out to him his usual complaints, asserting that no one would take their corn, even for nothing, that the people had got quite out of all habits of obedience, and that probably the end of the world was coming soon. 'Fancy,' he wrote, among other things, 'my last coachman, the Kalmuck boy, do you remember him? has been bewitched, and the fellow would certainly have died, and I should have had none to drive me, but, thank goodness, some kind folks suggested and advised to send the sick man to Ryazan, to a priest, well-known as a master against witchcraft: and his cure has actually succeeded as well as possible, in confirmation of which I lay before you the letter of the good father as a document.' Litvinov ran through this document with curiosity. In it was set forth: 'that the serving-man Nicanor Dmitriev was beset with a malady which could not be touched by the medical faculty; and this malady was the work of wicked people; but he himself, Nicanor, was the cause of it, since he had not fulfilled his promise to a certain girl, and therefore by the aid of others she had made him unfit for anything, and if I had not appeared to aid him in these circumstances, he would surely have perished utterly, like a worm; but I, trusting in the All-seeing Eye, have become a stay to him in his life; and how I accomplished it, that is a mystery; I beg your excellency not to countenance a girl who has such wicked arts, and even to chide her would be no harm, or she may again work him a mischief.'

Litvinov fell to musing over this document; it brought him a whiff of the desert, of the steppes, of the blind darkness of the life mouldering there, and it seemed a marvellous thing that he should be reading such a letter in Baden, of all places. Meanwhile it had long struck midnight; Litvinov went to bed and put out his light. But he could not get to sleep; the faces he had seen, the talk he had heard, kept coming back and revolving, strangely interwoven and entangled in his burning head, which ached from the fumes of tobacco. Now he seemed to hear Gubaryov's muttering, and fancied his eyes with their dull, persistent stare fastened on the floor; then suddenly those eyes began to glow and leap, and he recognised Madame Suhantchikov, and listened to her shrill voice, and involuntarily repeated after her in a whisper, 'she did, she did, slap his face.' Then the clumsy figure of Potugin passed before him; and for the tenth, and the twentieth time he went over every word he had uttered; then, like a jack in the box, Voroshilov jumped up in his trim coat, which fitted him like a new uniform; and Pishtchalkin gravely and sagaciously nodded his well-cut and truly well-intentioned head; and then Bindasov bawled and swore, and Bambaev fell into tearful transports. . . . And above all—this scent, this persistent, sweet, heavy scent gave him no rest, and grew more and more powerful in the darkness, and more and more importunately it reminded him of something which still eluded his grasp. . . . The idea occurred to Litvinov that the scent of flowers at night in a bedroom was injurious, and he got up, and groping his way to the nosegay, carried it into the next room; but even from there the oppressive fragrance penetrated to him on his pillow and under the counterpane, and he tossed in misery from side to side. A slight delirium had already begun to creep over him; already the priest, 'the master against witchcraft' had twice run across his road in the guise of a very playful hare with a beard and a pig-tail, and Voroshilov was trilling before him, sitting in a huge general's plumed cock-hat like a nightingale in a bush. . . . When suddenly he jumped up in bed, and clasping his hands, cried, ' Can it be she ? it can't be ! '

But to explain this exclamation of Litvinov's we must beg the indulgent reader to go back a few years with us.

VII

EARLY in the fifties, there was living in Moscow, in very straitened circumstances, almost in poverty, the numerous family of the Princes Osinin. These were real princes—not Tartar-Georgians, but pure-blooded descendants of Rurik. Their name is often to be met with in our chronicles under the first grand princes of Moscow, who created a united Russia. They possessed wide acres and many domains. Many a time they were rewarded for 'service and blood and disablement.' They sat in the Council of Boyars. One of them even rose to a very high position. But they fell under the ban of the empire through the plots of enemies 'on a charge of witchcraft and evil philtres,' and they were ruined 'terribly and beyond recall.' They were deprived of their rank, and banished to remote parts; the Osinins fell and had never risen again, had never attained to power again. The ban was taken off in time, and they were even reinstated in their Moscow house and belongings, but it was of no avail. Their family was impoverished, 'run to seed'; it did not revive under Peter, nor under Catherine; and constantly dwindling and growing humbler, it had by now reckoned private stewards, managers of wine-shops, and ward police-inspectors among its members. The family of Osinins, of whom we have made mention, consisted of a husband and wife and five children. It was living near the Dogs' Place, in a one-storied little wooden house, with a striped portico looking on to the street, green lions on the gates, and all the other pretensions of nobility, though it could hardly make both ends meet, was constantly in debt at the green-grocer's, and often sitting without firewood or candles in the winter. The prince himself was a dull, indolent man, who had once been a handsome dandy, but had gone to seed completely. More from regard for his wife, who had been a maid-of-honour, than from respect for his name, he had been presented with one of those old-fashioned Moscow posts that have a small salary, a queer-sounding name, and absolutely no duties attached. He never meddled in anything, and did nothing but smoke from morning till night, breathing heavily, and always wrapped in a dressing-gown. His wife was a sickly irritable woman, for ever worried over domestic trifles — over getting her children placed in government schools, and keeping up her Petersburg connections; she could never accustom herself to her position and her remoteness from the Court.

Litvinov's father had made acquaintance with the Osinins during his residence at Moscow, had had occasion to do them some services, and had once lent them three hundred roubles; and his son often visited them while he was a student; his lodging happened to be at no great distance from their house. But he was not drawn to them simply as near neighbours, nor tempted by their comfortless way of living. He began to be a frequent visitor at their house after he had fallen in love with their eldest daughter Irina.

She had then completed her seventeenth year; she had only just left school, from which her mother withdrew her through a disagreement with the principal. This disagreement arose from the fact that Irina was to have delivered at a public function some verses in French, complimentary to the curator, and just before the performance her place was filled by another girl, the daughter of a very rich spirit-contractor. The princess could not stomach this affront; and indeed Irina herself never forgave the principal for this act of injustice; she had been dreaming beforehand of how she would rise before the eyes of every one, attracting universal attention, and would deliver her speech, and how Moscow would talk about her afterwards! . . . And, indeed, Moscow would have talked about her afterwards. She was a tall, slim girl, with a somewhat hollow chest and narrow unformed shoulders, with a skin of a dead-white, rare at her age, and pure and smooth as china, with thick fair hair; there were darker tresses mingled in a very original way with the light ones. Her features — exquisitely, almost too perfectly, correct — had not yet quite lost the innocent expression that belongs to childhood; the languid curves of her lovely neck, and her smile — half-indifferent, half-weary — betrayed the nervous temperament of a delicate girl; but in the lines of those fine, faintly-smiling lips, of that small, falcon, slightly-narrow nose, there was something wilful and passionate, something dangerous for herself and others. Astounding, really astounding were her eyes, dark grey with greenish lights, languishing, almond-shaped as an Egyptian goddess's, with shining lashes and bold sweep of eyebrow. There was a strange look in those eyes; they seemed looking out intently and thoughtfully—looking out from some unknown depth and distance. At school, Irina had been reputed one of the best pupils for intelligence and abilities, but of uneven temper, fond of power, and headstrong; one class-mistress prophesied that her passions would be her ruin—'*vos passions vous perdront*'; on the other hand, another class-mistress censured her for coldness and want of feeling, and called her '*une jeune fille sans cœur.*' Irina's companions thought her proud and reserved: her brothers and sisters stood a little in awe of her: her mother had no confidence in her: and her father felt ill at ease when she fastened her mysterious eyes upon him. But she inspired a feeling of involuntary respect in both her father and her mother, not so much through her qualities, as from a peculiar, vague sense of expectations which she had, in some undefined way, awakened in them.

'You will see, Praskovya Danilovna,' said the old prince one day, taking his pipe out of his mouth, 'our chit of an Irina will give us all a lift in the world yet.'

The princess got angry, and told her husband that he made use of '*des expressions insupportables*'; afterwards, however, she fell to musing over his words, and repeated through her teeth:

'Well .. and it would be a good thing if we did get a lift.'

Irina enjoyed almost unlimited freedom in her parents' house; they did not spoil her, they even avoided her a little, but they did not thwart her, and that was all she wanted. . . . Sometimes—during some too humiliating scene—when some tradesman would come and keep shouting, to be heard over the whole court, that he was sick of coming after his money, or their own servants would begin abusing their masters to their face, with 'fine princes you are, to be sure; you may whistle for your supper, and go hungry to bed'—Irina would not stir a muscle; she would sit unmoved, an evil smile on her dark face; and her smile alone was more bitter to her parents than any reproaches, and they felt themselves guilty—guilty, though guiltless—towards this being on whom had been bestowed, as it seemed, from her very birth, the right to wealth, to luxury, and to homage.

Litvinov fell in love with Irina from the moment he saw her (he was only three years older than she was), but for a long while he failed to obtain not only a response, but even a hearing. Her manner to him was even overcast with a shade of something like hostility; he did in fact wound her pride, and she concealed the wound, and could never forgive it. He was too young and too modest at that time to understand what might be concealed under this hostile, almost contemptuous severity. Often, forgetful of lectures and exercises, he would sit and sit in the Osinins' cheerless drawing-room, stealthily watching Irina, his heart slowly and painfully throbbing and suffocating him; and she would seem angry or bored, would get up and walk about the room, look coldly at him as though he were a table or chair, shrug her shoulders, and fold her arms. Or for a whole evening, even when talking with Litvinov, she would purposely avoid looking at him, as though denying him even that grace. Or she would at last take up a book and stare at it, not reading, but frowning and biting her lips. Or else she would suddenly ask her father or brother aloud: 'What's the German for patience?' He tried to tear himself away from the enchanted circle in which he suffered and struggled impotently like a bird in a trap; he went away from Moscow for a week. He nearly went out of his mind with misery and dulness; he returned quite thin and ill to the Osinins'. . . . Strange to say, Irina too had grown perceptibly thinner during those days; her face had grown pale, her cheeks were wan. . . . But she met him with still greater coldness, with almost malignant indifference; as though he had intensified that secret wound he had dealt at her pride. . . . She tortured him in this way for two months. Then everything was transformed in one day. It was as though love had broken into flame with the heat, or had dropped down from a storm-cloud. One day —long will he remember that day—he was once more sitting in the Osinins' drawing-room at the window, and was looking mechanically into the street. There was vexation and weariness in his heart, he despised himself, and yet he could not move from his place. . . He thought that if a river ran there under the window, he would throw himself in, with a shudder of fear, but without a regret. Irina placed herself not far from him, and was somehow strangely silent and motionless. For some days now she had not talked to him at all, or to any one else; she kept sitting, leaning on her elbows, as though she were in perplexity, and only rarely she looked slowly round. This cold torture was at last more than Litvinov could bear; he got up, and without saying good-bye, he began to look for his hat. 'Stay,' sounded suddenly, in a soft whisper. Litvinov's heart throbbed, he did not at once recognise Irina's voice; in that one word, there was a ring of something that had never been in it before. He lifted his head and was stupefied; Irina was looking fondly—yes, fondly at him. 'Stay,' she repeated; 'don't go. I want to be with you.' Her voice sank still lower. 'Don't go. . . . I wish it.' Understanding nothing, not fully conscious what he was doing, he drew near her, stretched out his hands. . . . She gave him both of hers at once, then smiling, flushing hotly, she turned away, and still smiling, went out of the room. She came back a few minutes later with her youngest sister, looked at him again with the same prolonged tender gaze, and made him sit near her. . . . At first she could say nothing; she only sighed and blushed; then she began, timidly as it were, to question him about his pursuits, a thing she had never done before. In the evening of the same day, she tried several times to beg his forgiveness for not having done him justice before, assured him she had now become quite different, astonished him by a sudden outburst of republicanism (he had at that time a positive hero-worship for Robespierre, and did not presume to criticise Marat aloud), and only a week later he knew that she loved him. Yes; he long remembered that first day . . . but he did not forget those that came after either—those days, when still forcing himself to doubt, afraid to believe in it, he saw clearly, with transports of rapture, almost of dread, bliss unhoped for coming to life, growing, irresistibly carrying everything before it, reaching him at last. Then followed the radiant moments of first love—moments which are not destined to be, and could not fittingly be, repeated in the same life. Irina became all at once as docile as a lamb, as soft as silk, and boundlessly kind; she began giving lessons to her younger sisters—not on the piano, she was no musician, but in French and English; she read their school-books with them, and looked after the housekeeping; everything was amusing and interesting to her; she would sometimes chatter incessantly, and sometimes sink into speechless tenderness; she made all sorts of plans, and was lost in endless anticipations of what she would do when she was married to Litvinov (they never doubted that their marriage would come to pass), and how together they would . . . 'Work?' prompted Litvinov. . . . 'Yes; work,' repeated Irina, 'and read . . . but travel before all things.' She particularly wanted to leave Moscow as soon as possible, and when Litvinov reminded her that he had not yet finished his course of study at the university, she always replied, after a moment's thought, that it was quite possible to finish his studies at Berlin or . . . somewhere or other. Irina was very little reserved in the expression of her feelings, and so her relations with Litvinov did not long remain a secret from the prince and princess. Rejoice they could not; but, taking all circumstances into consideration, they saw no necessity for putting a veto on it at once. Litvinov's fortune was considerable. . . .

'But his family, his family!' . . . protested the princess. 'Yes, his family, of course,' replied the prince; 'but at least he's not quite a plebeian; and, what's the principal point, Irina, you know, will not listen to us. Has there ever been a time when she did not do what she chose? *Vous connaissez sa violence!* Besides, there is nothing fixed definitely yet.' So reasoned the prince, but mentally he added, however: 'Madame Litvinov—is that all? I had expected something else.' Irina took complete possession of her future *fiancé*, and indeed he himself eagerly surrendered himself into her hands. It was as if he had fallen into a rapid river, and had lost himself. . . . And bitter and sweet it was to him, and he regretted nothing and heeded nothing. To reflect on the significance and the duties of marriage, or whether he, so hopelessly enslaved, could be a good husband, and what sort of wife Irina would make, and whether their relations to one another were what they should be—was more than he could bring himself to. His blood was on fire, he could think of nothing, only—to follow her, be with her, for the future without end, and then—let come what may!

But in spite of the complete absence of

opposition on Litvinov's side, and the wealth of impulsive tenderness on Irina's, they did not get on quite without any misunderstandings and quarrels. One day he ran to her straight from the university in an old coat and ink-stained hands. She rushed to meet him with her accustomed fond welcome; suddenly she stopped short.

'You have no gloves,' she said abruptly, and added directly after: 'Fie! what a student you are!'

'You are too particular, Irina,' remarked Litvinov.

'You are a regular student,' she repeated. '*Vous n'êtes pas distingué*'; and turning her back on him she went out of the room. It is true that an hour later she begged him to forgive her. . . . As a rule she readily censured herself and accused herself to him; but, strange to say, she often almost with tears blamed herself for evil propensities which she had not, and obstinately denied her real defects. Another time he found her in tears, her head in her hands, and her hair in disorder; and when, all in agitation, he asked her the cause of her grief, she pointed with her finger at her own bosom without speaking. Litvinov gave an involuntary shiver. 'Consumption!' flashed through his brain, and he seized her hand.

'Are you ill, Irina?' he articulated in a shaking voice. (They had already begun on great occasions to call each other by their first names.) 'Let me go at once for a doctor.'

But Irina did not let him finish; she stamped with her foot in vexation.

'I am perfectly well. . . . but this dress . . . don't you understand?'

'What is it? . . . this dress,' he repeated in bewilderment.

'What is it? Why, that I have no other, and that it is old and disgusting, and I am obliged to put on this dress every day . . . even when you—Grisha—Grigory, come here. . . . You will leave off loving me, at last, seeing me so slovenly!'

'For goodness sake, Irina, what are you saying? That dress is very nice. . . . It is dear to me too because I saw you for the first time in it, darling.'

Irina blushed.

'Do not remind me, if you please, Grigory Mihalovitch, that I had no other dress even then.'

'But I assure you, Irina Pavlovna, it suits you so exquisitely.'

'No, it is horrid, horrid,' she persisted, nervously pulling at her long, soft curls. 'Ugh, this poverty, poverty and squalor! How is one to escape from this sordidness! How get out of this squalor!'

Litvinov did not know what to say, and slightly turned away from her.

All at once Irina jumped up from her chair, and laid both her hands on his shoulders.

'But you love me, Grisha? You love me?' she murmured, putting her face close to him, and her eyes, still filled with tears, sparkled with the light of happiness, 'You love me, dear, even in this horrid dress?'

Litvinov flung himself on his knees before her.

'Ah, love me, love me, my sweet, my saviour,' she whispered, bending over him.

So the days flew, the weeks passed, and though as yet there had been no formal declaration, though Litvinov still deferred his demand for her hand, not, certainly, at his own desire, but awaiting directions from Irina (she remarked sometimes that they were both ridiculously young, and they must add at least a few weeks more to their years), still everything was moving to a conclusion, and the future as it came nearer grew more and more clearly defined, when suddenly an event occurred, which scattered all their dreams and plans like light roadside dust.

VIII

THAT winter the court visited Moscow. One festivity followed another; in its turn came the customary great ball in the Hall of Nobility. The news of this ball, only, it is true, in the form of an announcement in the *Political Gazette*, reached even the little house in Dogs' Place. The prince was the first to be roused by it; he decided at once that he must not fail to go and take Irina, that it would be unpardonable to let slip the opportunity of seeing their sovereigns, that for the old nobility this constituted indeed a duty in its own way. He defended his opinion with a peculiar warmth, not habitual in him; the princess agreed with him to some extent, and only sighed over the expense; but a resolute opposition was displayed by Irina. 'It is not necessary, I will not go,' she replied to all her parents' arguments. Her obstinacy reached such proportions that the old prince decided at last to beg Litvinov to try to persuade her, by reminding her among other reasons that it was not proper for a young girl to avoid society, that she ought to 'have this experience,' that no one ever saw her anywhere, as it was. Litvinov undertook to lay these 'reasons' before her. Irina looked steadily and scrutinisingly at him, so steadily and scrutinisingly that he was confused, and then, playing with the ends of her sash, she said calmly:

'Do you desire it, you?'

'Yes. . . . I suppose so,' replied Litvinov hesitatingly. 'I agree with your papa. . . . Indeed, why should you not go . . to see the world, and show yourself,' he added with a short laugh.

'To show myself,' she repeated slowly. 'Very well then, I will go. . . . Only remember, it is you yourself who desired it.'

'That's to say, I——.' Litvinov was beginning.

'You yourself have desired it,' she interposed. 'And here is one condition more; you must promise me that you will not be at this ball.'

'But why?'

'I wish it to be so.'

Litvinov unclasped his hands.

'I submit . . . but I confess I should so have enjoyed seeing you in all your grandeur, witnessing the sensation you are certain to make. . . . How proud I should be of you!' he added with a sigh.

Irina laughed.

'All the grandeur will consist of a white frock, and as for the sensation. . . . Well, any way, I wish it.'

'Irina, darling, you seem to be angry?'

Irina laughed again.

'Oh, no! I am not angry. Only, Grisha . . . (She fastened her eyes on him, and he thought he had never before seen such an expression in them.) 'Perhaps, it must be,' she added in an undertone.

'But, Irina, you love me, dear?'

'I love you,' she answered with almost solemn gravity, and she clasped his hand firmly like a man.

All the following days Irina was busily occupied over her dress and her coiffure; on the day before the ball she felt unwell, she could not sit still, and twice she burst into tears in solitude; before Litvinov she wore the same uniform smile. . . . She treated him, however, with her old tenderness, but carelessly, and was constantly looking at herself in the glass. On the day of the ball she was silent and pale, but collected. At nine o'clock in the evening Litvinov came to look at her. When she came to meet him in a white tarlatan gown, with a spray of small blue flowers in her slightly raised hair, he almost uttered a cry; she seemed to him so lovely and stately beyond what was natural to her years. 'Yes, she has grown up since this morning!' he thought, 'and how she holds herself! That's what race does!' Irina stood before him, her hands hanging loose, without smiles or affectation, and looked resolutely, almost boldly, not at him, but away into the distance straight before her.

'You are just like a princess in a story book,' said Litvinov at last. 'You are like a warrior before the battle, before victory.... You did not allow me to go to this ball,' he went on, while she remained motionless as before, not because she was not listening to him, but because she was following another inner voice, 'but you will not refuse to accept and take with you these flowers?'

He offered her a bunch of heliotrope. She looked quickly at Litvinov, stretched out her hand, and suddenly seizing the end of the spray which decorated her hair, she said:

'Do you wish it, Grisha? Only say the word, and I will tear off all this, and stop at home.'

Litvinov's heart seemed fairly bursting. Irina's hand had already snatched the spray....

'No, no, what for?' he interposed hurriedly, in a rush of generous and magnanimous feeling, 'I am not an egoist.... Why should I restrict your freedom ... when I know that your heart —— '

'Well, don't come near me, you will crush my dress,' she said hastily.

Litvinov was disturbed.

'But you will take the nosegay?' he asked.

'Of course; it is very pretty, and I love that scent. *Merci*—I shall keep it in memory——'

'Of your first coming out,' observed Litvinov, 'your first triumph.'

Irina looked over her shoulder at herself in the glass, scarcely bending her figure.

'And do I really look so nice? You are not partial?'

Litvinov overflowed in enthusiastic praises. Irina was already not listening to him, and holding the flowers up to her face, she was again looking away into the distance with her strange, as it were, overshadowed, dilated eyes, and the ends of her delicate ribbons stirred by a faint current of air rose slightly behind her shoulders like wings.

The prince made his appearance, his hair well becurled, in a white tie, and a shabby black evening coat, with the medal of nobility on a Vladimir ribbon in his buttonhole. After him came the princess in a china silk dress of antique cut, and with the anxious severity under which mothers try to conceal their agitation, set her daughter to rights behind, that is to say, quite needlessly shook out the folds of her gown. An antiquated hired coach with seats for four, drawn by two shaggy hacks, crawled up to the steps, its wheels grating over the frozen mounds of unswept snow, and a decrepit groom in a most unlikely-looking livery came running out of the passage, and with a sort of desperate courage announced that the carriage was ready. . . . After giving a blessing for the night to the children left at home, and enfolding themselves in their fur wraps, the prince and princess went out to the steps; Irina in a little cloak, too thin and too short—how she hated the little cloak at that moment!—followed them in silence. Litvinov escorted them outside, hoping for a last look from Irina, but she took her seat in the carriage without turning her head.

About midnight he walked under the windows of the Hall of Nobility. Countless lights of huge candelabra shone with brilliant radiance through the red curtains; and the whole square, blocked with carriages, was ringing with the insolent, festive, seductive strains of a waltz of Strauss.'

The next day at one o'clock, Litvinov betook himself to the Osinins'. He found no one at home but the prince, who informed him at once that Irina had a headache, that she was in bed, and would not get up till the evening, that such an indisposition was however little to be wondered at after a first ball.

'*C'est très naturel, vous savez, dans les jeunes filles,*' he added in French, somewhat to Litvinov's surprise; the latter observed at the same instant that the prince was not in his dressing-gown as usual, but was wearing a coat. 'And besides,' continued Osinin, 'she may well be a little upset after the events of yesterday!'

'Events?' muttered Litvinov.

'Yes, yes, events, events, *de vrais événements.* You cannot imagine, Grigory Mihalovitch, *quel succès elle a eu*! The whole court noticed her! Prince Alexandr Fedorovitch said that her place was not here, and that she reminded him of Countess Devonshirse. You know ... that ... celebrated. ... And old Blazenkrampf declared in the hearing of all, that Irina was *la reine du bal*, and desired to be introduced to her; he was introduced to me too, that's to say, he told me that he remembered me a hussar, and asked me where I was holding office now. Most entertaining man that Count, and such an *adorateur du beau sexe*! But that's not all; my princess ... they gave her no peace either: Natalya Nikitishna herself conversed with her ... what more could we have? Irina danced *avec tous les meilleurs cavaliers*; they kept bringing them up to me. . . . I positively lost count of them. Would you believe it, they were all flocking about us in crowds; in the mazurka they did nothing but seek her out. One foreign diplomatist, hearing she was a Moscow girl, said to the Tsar: 'Sire,' he said, '*décidément c'est Moscou qui est le centre de votre empire!*' and another diplomatist added: '*C'est une vraie révolution, Sire—révélation* or *révolution* . . . something of that sort. Yes, yes, it was. I tell you it was something extraordinary.'

'Well, and Irina Pavlovna herself?' inquired Litvinov, whose hands and feet had grown cold hearing the prince's speech, 'did she enjoy herself, did she seem pleased?'

'Of course she enjoyed herself; how could she fail to be pleased? But, as you know, she's not to be seen through at a glance! Every one was saying to me yesterday: it is really surprising! *jamais on ne dirait que mademoiselle votre fille est à son premier bal.* Count Reisenbach among the rest . . . you know him most likely.'

'No, I don't know him at all, and have never heard of him.'

'My wife's cousin.'

'I don't know him.'

'A rich man, a chamberlain, living in Petersburg, in the swim of things; in Livonia every one is in his hands. Hitherto he has neglected us . . . but there, I don't bear him ill-will for that. *J'ai l'humeur facile, comme vous savez.* Well, that's the kind of man he is. He sat near Irina, conversed with her for a quarter of an hour, not more, and said afterwards to my princess: "*Ma cousine,*" he says, "*votre fille est une perle; c'est une perfection,* every one is congratulating me on such a niece. . . ." And afterwards I look round—and he had gone up to a . . . a very great personage, and was talking, and kept looking at Irina . . . and the personage was looking at her too.' . . .

'And so Irina Pavlovna will not appear all day?' Litvinov asked again.

'Quite so; her head aches very badly. She told me to greet you from her, and thank you for your flowers, *qu'on a trouvé charmant.* She needs rest. . . . The princess has gone out on a round of visits . . . and I myself . . . you see. . . .'

The prince cleared his throat, and began to fidget as though he were at a loss what to add further. Litvinov took his hat, and saying he did not want to disturb him, and would call again later to inquire after her health, he went away.

A few steps from the Osinins' house he saw an elegant carriage for two persons standing before the police sentry-box. A groom in livery, equally elegant, was bending negligently from the box, and inquiring of the Finnish police-sergeant whereabouts Prince Pavel Vassilyevitch Osinin lived. Litvinov glanced at the carriage; in it sat a middle-aged man of bloated complexion, with a wrinkled and haughty face, a Greek nose, and an evil mouth, muffled in a sable wrap, by all outward signs a very great man indeed

IX

LITVINOV did not keep his promise of returning later; he reflected that it would be better to defer his visit till the following day. When he went into the too familiar drawing-room at about twelve o'clock, he found there the two youngest princesses, Viktorinka and Kleopatrinka. He greeted them, and then inquired, 'Was Irina Pavlovna better, and could he see her?'

'Irinotchka has gone away with mammy,' replied Viktorinka; she lisped a little, but was more forward than her sister.

'How . . . gone away?' repeated Litvinov, and there was a sort of still shudder in the very bottom of his heart. 'Does she not, does she not look after you about this time, and give you your lessons?'

'Irinotchka will not give us any lessons any more now,' answered Viktorinka. 'Not any more now,' Kleopatrinka repeated after her.

'Is your papa at home?' asked Litvinov.

'Papa is not at home,' continued Viktorinka, 'and Irinotchka is not well; all night long she was crying and crying....'

'Crying?'

'Yes, crying... Yegorovna told me, and her eyes are so red, they are quite in-in-flamed....'

Litvinov walked twice up and down the room shuddering as though with cold, and went back to his lodging. He experienced a sensation like that which gains possession of a man when he looks down from a high tower; everything failed within him, and his head was swimming slowly with a sense of nausea. Dull stupefaction, and thoughts scurrying like mice, vague terror, and the numbness of expectation, and curiosity—strange, almost malignant—and the weight of crushed tears in his heavy laden breast, on his lips the forced empty smile, and a meaningless prayer—addressed to no one.... Oh, how bitter it all was, and how hideously degrading! 'Irina does not want to see me,' was the thought that was incessantly revolving in his brain; 'so much is clear; but why is it? What can have happened at that ill-fated ball? And how is such a change possible all at once? So suddenly....' People always see death coming suddenly, but they can never get accustomed to its suddenness, they feel it senseless. 'She sends no message for me, does not want to explain herself to me. . . .'

'Grigory Mihalitch,' called a strained voice positively in his ear.

Litvinov started, and saw before him his servant with a note in his hand. He recognised Irina's writing. . . . Before he had broken the seal, he had a foreknowledge of woe, and bent his head on his breast and hunched his shoulders, as though shrinking from the blow.

He plucked up courage at last, and tore open the envelope all at once. On a small sheet of notepaper were the following lines:

'Forgive me, Grigory Mihalitch. All is over between us; I am going away to Petersburg. I am dreadfully unhappy, but the thing is done. It seems my fate . . . but no, I do not want to justify myself. My presentiments have been realised. Forgive me, forget me; I am not worthy of you.—Irina. Be magnanimous: do not try to see me.'

Litvinov read these five lines, and slowly dropped on to the sofa, as though some one had dealt him a blow on the breast. He dropped the note, picked it up, read it again, whispered 'to Petersburg,' and dropped it again; that was all. There even came upon him a sense of peace; he even, with his hands thrown behind him, smoothed the pillow under his head.

'Men wounded to death don't fling themselves about,' he thought, 'as it has come, so it has gone. All this is natural enough : I always expected it. . . .' (He was lying to himself; he had never expected anything like it.) 'Crying? . . . Was she crying? . . . What was she crying for? Why, she did not love me! But all that is easily understood and in accordance with her character. She—she is not worthy of me. . . . That's it!' (He laughed bitterly.) 'She did not know herself what power was latent in her,—well, convinced of it in her effect at the ball, was it likely she would stay with an insignificant student?—all that's easily understood.'

But then he remembered her tender words, her smile, and those eyes, those never to be forgotten eyes, which he would never see again, which used to shine and melt at simply meeting his eyes ; he recalled one swift, timorous, burning kiss—and suddenly he fell to sobbing, sobbing convulsively, furiously, vindictively ; turned over on his face, and choking and stifling with frenzied satisfaction as though thirsting to tear himself to pieces with all around him, he turned his hot face in the sofa pillow, and bit it in his teeth.

Alas! the gentleman whom Litvinov had seen the day before in the carriage was no other than the cousin of the Princess Osinin, the rich chamberlain, Count Reisenbach. Noticing the sensation produced by Irina on certain personages of the highest rank, and instantaneously reflecting what advantages might *mit etwas Accuratesse* be derived from the fact, the count made his plan at once like a man of energy and a skilful courtier. He decided to act swiftly, in Napoleonic style. 'I will take that original girl into my house,' was what he meditated, 'in Petersburg; I will make her my heiress, devil take me, of my whole property even; as I have no children. She is my niece, and my countess is dull all alone. .. It's always more agreeable to have a pretty face in one's drawing-room. ... Yes, yes; ... that's it; *es ist eine Idee, es ist eine Idee!*' He would have to dazzle, bewilder, and impress the parents. 'They've not enough to eat'—the count pursued his reflection when he was in the carriage and on his way to Dogs' Place—'so, I warrant, they won't be obstinate. They're not such over-sentimental folks either. I might give them a sum of money down into the bargain. And she? She will consent. Honey is sweet—she had a taste of it last night. It's a whim on my part, granted; let them profit by it, ... the fools. I shall say to them one thing and another ... and you must decide—otherwise

I shall adopt another — an orphan — which would be still more suitable. Yes or no — twenty-four hours I fix for the term — *und damit Punctum.*'

And with these very words on his lips, the count presented himself before the prince, whom he had forewarned of his visit the evening before at the ball. On the result of this visit it seems hardly worth while to enlarge further. The count was not mistaken in his prognostications: the prince and princess were in fact not obstinate, and accepted the sum of money; and Irina did in fact consent before the allotted term had expired. It was not easy for her to break off her relations with Litvinov; she loved him; and after sending him her note, she almost kept her bed, weeping continually, and grew thin and wan. But for all that, a month later the princess carried her off to Petersburg, and established her at the count's; committing her to the care of the countess, a very kind-hearted woman, but with the brain of a hen, and something of a hen's exterior.

Litvinov threw up the university, and went home to his father in the country. Little by little his wound healed. At first he had no news of Irina, and indeed he avoided all conversation that touched on Petersburg and Petersburg society. Later on, by degrees, rumours—not evil exactly, but curious—began to circulate about her; gossip began to be busy about her. The name of the young Princess Osinin, encircled in splendour, impressed with quite a special stamp, began to be more and more frequently mentioned even in provincial circles. It was pronounced with curiosity, respect, and envy, as men at one time used to mention the name of the Countess Vorotinsky. At last the news came of her marriage. But Litvinov hardly paid attention to these last tidings; he was already betrothed to Tatyana.

Now, the reader can no doubt easily understand exactly what it was Litvinov recalled when he cried, 'Can it be she?' and therefore we will return to Baden and take up again the broken thread of our story.

X

LITVINOV fell asleep very late, and did not sleep long; the sun had only just risen when he got out of bed. The summits of dark mountains visible from his windows stood out in misty purple against the clear sky. 'How cool it must be there under the trees!' he thought; and he dressed in haste, and looked with indifference at the bouquet which had opened more luxuriantly after the night; he took a stick and set off towards the 'Old Castle' on the famous 'Cliffs.' Invigorating and soothing was the caressing contact of the fresh morning about him. He drew long breaths, and stepped out boldly; the vigorous health of youth was throbbing in every vein; the very earth seemed springy under his light feet. With every step he grew more light-hearted, more happy; he walked in the dewy shade in the thick sand of the little paths, beside the fir-trees that were fringed with the vivid green of the spring shoots at the end of every twig. 'How jolly it is!' he kept repeating to himself. Suddenly he heard the sound of familiar voices; he looked ahead and saw Voroshilov and Bambaev coming to meet him. The sight of them jarred upon him; he rushed away like a school-boy avoiding his teacher, and hid himself behind a bush. . . 'My Creator!' he prayed, 'mercifully remove my countrymen!' He felt that he would not have grudged any money at the moment if only they did not see him. . . . And they actually did not see him: the Creator was merciful to him. Voroshilov, in his self-confident military voice, was holding forth to Bambaev on the various phases of Gothic architecture, and Bambaev only grunted approvingly; it was obvious that Voroshilov had been dinning his phrases into him a long while, and the good-natured enthusiast was beginning to be bored. Compressing his lips and craning his neck, Litvinov listened a long while to their retreating footsteps; for a long time the accents of instructive discourse—now guttural, now nasal—reached his ears; at last, all was still again. Litvinov breathed freely, came out of his ambush, and walked on.

For three hours he wandered about the mountains. Sometimes he left the path, and jumped from rock to rock, slipping now and then on the smooth moss; then he would sit down on a fragment of the cliff under an oak or a beech, and muse on pleasant fancies to the never-ceasing gurgle of the little rills overgrown with ferns, the soothing rustle of the leaves, and the shrill notes of a solitary blackbird. A light and equally pleasant drowsiness began to steal over him, it seemed to approach him caressingly, and he dropped asleep . . . but suddenly he smiled and looked round; the gold and green of the forest, and the moving foliage beat down softly on his eyes—and again he smiled and again closed them. He began to want breakfast, and he made his way towards the old castle where for a few kreutzers he could get a glass of good milk and coffee. But he had hardly had time to establish himself at one of the little white-painted tables set on the platform before the castle, when the heavy tramping of horses was heard, and three open carriages drove up, out of which stepped a rather numerous company of ladies and gentlemen. . . . Litvinov at once recognised them as Russians, though they were all talking French . . . just because they were all talking French. The ladies' dresses were marked by a studied elegance; the gentlemen wore close-fitting coats with waists—which is not altogether usual nowadays—grey trousers of fancy material, and very glossy town hats. A narrow black cravat closely fettered the neck of each of these gentlemen, and something military was apparent in their whole deportment. They were, in fact, military men; Litvinov had chanced upon a picnic party of young generals—persons of the highest society, of weight and importance. Their importance was clearly expressed in everything: in their discreet nonchalance, in their amiably condescending smiles, in the intense indifference of their expression, the effeminate little movements of their shoulders, the swing of the figure, and the crook of the knees; it was expressed, too, in the sound of their voices, which seemed to be affably and fastidiously thanking a subservient multitude. All these officers were superlatively washed and shaved, and thoroughly saturated with that genuine aroma of nobility and the Guards, compounded of the best cigar smoke, and the most marvellous patchouli. They all had the hands too of noblemen—white and large, with nails firm as ivory; their moustaches seemed positively polished, their teeth shone, and their skin—rosy on their cheeks, bluish on their chins—was most delicate and fine. Some of the young generals were frivolous, others were serious; but the stamp of the best breeding was on all of them. Each of them seemed to be deeply conscious of his own dignity, and the importance of his own future part in the government, and conducted himself with severity and ease, with a faint shade of that carelessness, that 'deuce-take-it' air, which comes out so naturally during foreign travel. The party seated themselves with much noise and ostentation, and called the obsequious waiters. Litvinov made haste to drink off his glass of milk, paid for it, and putting his hat on, was just making off past the party of generals. . . .

'Grigory Mihalitch,' he heard a woman's voice. 'Don't you recognise me?'

He stopped involuntarily. That voice. . . . that voice had too often set his heart beating in the past. . . . He turned round and saw Irina.

She was sitting at a table, her arms folded on the back of a chair drawn up near; with her head bent on one side and a smile on her face, she was looking at him cordially, almost with delight.

Litvinov knew her at once, though she had changed since he saw her that last time ten years ago, though she had been transformed from a girl into a woman. Her slim figure had developed and reached its perfection, the lines of her once narrow shoulders now recalled the goddesses that stand out on the ceilings of ancient Italian palaces. But her eyes remained the same, and it seemed to Litvinov that they were looking at him just as in those days in the little house in Moscow.

'Irina Pavlovna,' he uttered irresolutely.

'You know me? How glad I am! how glad——'

She stopped short, slightly blushing, and drew herself up.

'This is a very pleasant meeting,' she continued now in French. 'Let me introduce you to my husband. *Valérien, Monsieur Litvinov, un ami d'enfance*; Valerian Vladimirovitch Ratmirov, my husband.'

One of the young generals, almost the most elegant of all, got up from his seat, and with excessive courtesy bowed to Litvinov, while the rest of his companions faintly knitted their brows, or rather each of them withdrew for an instant into himself, as though protesting betimes against any contact with an extraneous civilian, and the other ladies taking part in the picnic thought fit to screw up their eyes a little and simper, and even to assume an air of perplexity.

'Have you—er—been long in Baden?' asked General Ratmirov, with a dandified air utterly un-Russian. He obviously did not know what to talk about with the friend of his wife's childhood.

'No, not long!' replied Litvinov.

'And do you intend to stay long?' pursued the polite general.

'I have not made up my mind yet.'

'Ah! that is very delightful . . . very.'

The general paused. Litvinov, too, was speechless. Both held their hats in their hands and bending forward with a grin, gazed at the top of each other's heads.

'*Deux gendarmes un beau dimanche*,' began humming—out of tune of course, we have never come across a Russian nobleman who did not sing out of tune—a dull-eyed and yellow-faced general, with an expression of constant irritability on his face, as though he could not forgive himself for his own appearance. Among all his companions he alone had not the complexion of a rose.

'But why don't you sit down, Grigory Mihalitch,' observed Irina at last.

Litvinov obeyed and sat down.

'*I say, Valérien, give me some fire*,' remarked in English another general, also young, but already stout, with fixed eyes which seemed staring into the air, and thick silky whiskers, into which he slowly plunged his snow-white fingers. Ratmirov gave him a silver matchbox.

'*Avez vous des papiros?*' asked one of the ladies, with a lisp.

'*De vrais papelitos, comtesse.*'

'*Deux gendarmes un beau dimanche,*' the dull-eyed general hummed again, with intense exasperation.

'You must be sure to come and see us,' Irina was saying to Litvinov meantime; 'we are staying at the Hôtel de l'Europe. From four to six I am always at home. We have not seen each other for such a long time.'

Litvinov looked at Irina; she did not drop her eyes.

'Yes, Irina Pavlovna, it is a long time—ever since we were at Moscow.'

'At Moscow, yes, at Moscow,' she repeated abruptly. 'Come and see me, we will talk and recall old times. Do you know, Grigory Mihalitch, you have not changed much.'

'Really? But you have changed, Irina Pavlovna.'

'I have grown older.'

'No, I did not mean that.'

'*Irène?*' said a lady in a yellow hat and with yellow hair in an interrogative voice after some preliminary whispering and giggling with the officer sitting near her. '*Irène?*'

'I am older,' pursued Irina, without answering the lady, 'but I am not changed. No, no, I am changed in nothing.'

'*Deux gendarmes un beau dimanche!*' was

heard again. The irritable general only remembered the first line of the well-known ditty.

'It still pricks a little, your excellency,' observed the stout general with the whiskers, with a loud and broad intonation, apparently quoting from some amusing story, well-known to the whole *beau monde*, and with a short wooden laugh he again fell to staring into the air. All the rest of the party laughed too.

'What a sad dog you are, Boris!' observed Ratmirov in an undertone. He spoke in English and pronounced even the name 'Boris' as if it were English.

'*Irène?*' the lady in the yellow hat said inquiringly for the third time. Irina turned sharply round to her.

'*Eh bien? quoi? que me voulez-vous?*'

'*Je vous dirai plus tard*,' replied the lady, mincing. With a very unattractive exterior, she was for ever mincing and grimacing. Some wit said of her that she '*minaudait dans le vide*,' grimaced upon the desert air.'

Irina frowned and shrugged her shoulders impatiently. '*Mais que fait donc Monsieur Verdier? Pourquoi ne vient-il pas?*' cried one lady with that prolonged drawl which is the peculiarity of the Great Russian accent, and is so insupportable to French ears.

'Ah, voo, ah, voo, mossoo Verdew, mossoo Verdew,' sighed another lady, whose birthplace was Arzamass.

'*Tranquillisez-vous, mesdames*,' interposed Ratmirov. '*Monsieur Verdier m'a promis de venir se mettre à vos pieds.*'

'He, he, he!'—The ladies fluttered their fans.

The waiter brought some glasses of beer.

'*Baierisch-Bier?*' inquired the general with whiskers, assuming a bass voice, and affecting astonishment—'*Guten Morgen.*'

'Well? Is Count Pavel still there?' one young general inquired coldly and listlessly of another.

'Yes,' replied the other equally coldly, '*Mais c'est provisoire. Serge*, they say, will be put in his place.'

'Aha!' filtered the first through his teeth.

'Ah, yes,' filtered the second.

'I can't understand,' began the general who had hummed the song, 'I can't understand what induced Paul to defend himself—to bring forward all sorts of reasons. Certainly, he crushed the merchant pretty well, *il lui a fait rendre gorge* . . . well, and what of it? He may have had his own motives.'

'He was afraid . . . of being shown up in the newspapers,' muttered some one.

The irritable general grew hot.

'Well, it is too much! Newspapers! Shown up! If it depended on me, I would not let anything be printed in those papers but the taxes on meat or bread, and announcements of sales of boots or furs.'

'And gentlemen's properties up for auction,' put in Ratmirov.

'Possibly under present circumstances.... What a conversation, though, in Baden *au Vieux-Château.*'

'*Mais pas du tout! pas du tout!*' replied the lady in the yellow hat, '*j'adore les questions politiques.*'

'*Madame a raison,*' interposed another general with an exceedingly pleasant and girlish-looking face. 'Why should we avoid those questions ... even in Baden?'

As he said these words he looked urbanely at Litvinov and smiled condescendingly. 'A man of honour ought never under any circumstances to disown his convictions.. Don't you think so?'

'Of course,' rejoined the irritable general, darting a look at Litvinov, and as it were indirectly attacking him, 'but I don't see the necessity ...'

'No, no,' the condescending general interposed with the same mildness, 'your friend,

Valerian Vladimirovitch, just referred to the sale of gentlemen's estates. Well? Is not that a fact?'

'But it's impossible to sell them nowadays; nobody wants them!' cried the irritable general.

'Perhaps . . . perhaps. For that very reason we ought to proclaim that fact . . . that sad fact at every step. We are ruined . . . very good; we are beggared . . . there's no disputing about that; but we, the great owners, we still represent a principle . . . *un principe*. To preserve that principle is our duty. *Pardon, madame*, I think you dropped your handkerchief. When some, so to say, darkness has come over even the highest minds, we ought submissively to point out (the general held out his finger) with the finger of a citizen the abyss to which everything is tending. We ought to warn, we ought to say with respectful firmness, "turn back, turn back. . . . That is what we ought to say.'

'There's no turning back altogether, though,' observed Ratmirov moodily.

The condescending general only grinned.

'Yes, altogether, altogether, *mon très cher*. The further back the better.'

The general again looked courteously at Litvinov. The latter could not stand it.

'Are we to return as far as the Seven Boyars, your excellency?'

'Why not? I express my opinion without hesitation; we must undo . . yes . . . undo all that has been done.'

'And the emancipation of the serfs.'

'And the emancipation . . . as far as that is possible. *On est patriote ou on ne l'est pas.* "And freedom?" they say to me. Do you suppose that freedom is prized by the people? Ask them——'

'Just try,' broke in Litvinov, 'taking that freedom away again.'

'*Comment nommez-vous ce monsieur?*' whispered the general to Ratmirov.

'What are you discussing here?' began the stout general suddenly. He obviously played the part of the spoilt child of the party. 'Is it all about the newspapers? About penny-a-liners? Let me tell you a little anecdote of what happened to me with a scribbling fellow—such a lovely thing. I was told he had written a libel on me. Well, of course, I at once had him brought before me. They brought me the penny-a-liner. '"How was it," said I, "my dear chap, you came to write this libel? Was your patriotism too much for you?" "Yes, it was too much," says he. "Well," says I, "and do you like money?" "Yes," says he. Then, gentlemen, I gave him the knob of my cane to sniff at. "And do you like that, my angel?" "No," says he, "I don't like that." "But sniff it as you ought," says I, "my hands are clean." "I don't like it," says he, "and that's all." "But I like it very much, my angel," says I, "though not for myself. Do you understand that allegory, my treasure?" "Yes," says he. "Then mind and be a good boy for the future, and now here's a rouble sterling for you; go away and be grateful to me night and day," and so the scribbling chap went off.'

The general burst out laughing and again every one followed his example—every one except Irina, who did not even smile and looked darkly at the speaker.

The condescending general slapped Boris on the shoulder.

'That's all your invention, O friend of my bosom. . . . You threatening any one with a stick. . . . You haven't got a stick. *C'est pour faire rire ces dames.* For the sake of a good story. But that's not the point. I said just now that we must turn back completely. Understand me. I am not hostile to so-called progress, but all these universities and seminaries, and popular schools, these students, priests' sons, and commoners, all these small fry, *tout ce fond du sac, la petite propriété, pire que le prolétariat* (the general uttered this in a languishing, almost faint voice) *voilà ce qui m'effraie* . . . that's where one ought to draw the line, and make other people draw it too.' (Again he gave Litvinov a genial glance.) 'Yes, one must draw the line. Don't forget that among us no one makes any demand, no one is asking for anything. Local government, for instance—who asks for that? Do you ask for it? or you, or you? or you, *mesdames*? You rule not only yourselves but all of us, you know.' (The general's handsome face was lighted up by a smile of amusement.) 'My dear friends, why should we curry favour with the multitude. You like democracy, it flatters you, and serves your ends ... but you know it's a double weapon. It is better in the old way, as before ... far more secure. Don't deign to reason with the herd, trust in the aristocracy, in that alone is power. ... Indeed it will be better. And progress ... I certainly have nothing against progress. Only don't give us lawyers and sworn juries and elective officials ... only don't touch discipline, discipline before all things —you may build bridges, and quays, and hospitals, and why not light the streets with gas?'

'Petersburg has been set on fire from one end to the other, so there you have your progress!' hissed the irritable general.

'Yes, you're a mischievous fellow, I can see,' said the stout general, shaking his head lazily; 'you would do for a chief-prosecutor, but in my opinion *avec Orphée aux enfers le progrès a dit son dernier mot.*'

'*Vous dites toujours des bêtises*,' giggled the lady from Arzamass.

The general looked dignified.

'*Je ne suis jamais plus sérieux, madame, que quand je dis des bêtises.*'

'Monsieur Verdier has uttered that very phrase several times already,' observed Irina in a low voice.

'*De la poigne et des formes*,' cried the stout general, '*de la poigne surtout*. And to translate into Russian: be civil but don't spare your fists.'

'Ah, you're a rascal, an incorrigible rascal,' interposed the condescending general. '*Mesdames*, don't listen to him, please. A barking dog does not bite. He cares for nothing but flirtation.'

'That's not right, though, Boris,' began Ratmirov, after exchanging a glance with his wife, 'it's all very well to be mischievous, but that's going too far. Progress is a phenomenon of social life, and this is what we must not forget; it's a symptom. It's what we must watch.'

'All right, I say,' observed the stout general, wrinkling up his nose; 'we all know you are aiming at the ministry.'

'Not at all . . . the ministry indeed! But really one can't refuse to recognise things.'

Boris plunged his fingers again into his whiskers, and stared into the air.

'Social life is very important, because in the development of the people, in the destinies, so to speak, of the country——'

'*Valérien*,' interrupted Boris reprovingly, '*il y a des dames ici*. I did not expect this of you, or do you want to get on to a committee?'

'But they are all closed now, thank God,' put in the irritable general, and he began humming again '*Deux gendarmes un beau dimanche*.'

Ratmirov raised a cambric handkerchief to his nose and gracefully retired from the discussion; the condescending general repeated 'Rascal! rascal!' but Boris turned to the lady who 'grimaced upon the desert air' and without lowering his voice, or a change in the expression of his face, began to ply her with questions as to when 'she would reward his devotion,' as though he were desperately in love with her and suffering tortures on her account.

At every moment during this conversation Litvinov felt more and more ill at ease. His pride, his clean plebeian pride, was fairly in revolt.

What had he, the son of a petty official, in common with these military aristocrats of Petersburg? He loved everything they hated;

he hated everything they loved; he was only too vividly conscious of it, he felt it in every part of his being. Their jokes he thought dull, their tone intolerable, every gesture false; in the very smoothness of their speeches he detected a note of revolting contemptuousness—and yet he was, as it were, abashed before them, before these creatures, these enemies. 'Ugh! how disgusting! I am in their way, I am ridiculous to them,' was the thought that kept revolving in his head. 'Why am I stopping? Let me escape at once, at once.' Irina's presence could not retain him; she, too, aroused melancholy emotions in him. He got up from his seat and began to take leave.

'You are going already?' said Irina, but after a moment's reflection she did not press him to stay, and only extracted a promise from him that he would not fail to come and see her. General Ratmirov took leave of him with the same refined courtesy, shook hands with him and accompanied him to the end of the platform. . . . But Litvinov had scarcely had time to turn round the first bend in the road when he heard a general roar of laughter behind him. This laughter had no reference to him, but was occasioned by the long-expected Monsieur Verdier, who suddenly made his appearance on the platform, in a Tyrolese hat, and blue blouse, riding a donkey, but the blood fairly rushed into Litvinov's cheeks, and he felt intense bitterness: his tightly compressed lips seemed as though drawn by wormwood. 'Despicable, vulgar creatures,' he muttered, without reflecting that the few minutes he had spent in their company had not given him sufficient ground for such severe criticism. And this was the world into which Irina had fallen, Irina, once his Irina! In this world she moved, and lived, and reigned; for it, she had sacrificed her personal dignity, the noblest feelings of her heart. . . . It was clearly as it should be; it was clear that she had deserved no better fate! How glad he was that she had not thought of questioning him about his intentions! He might have opened his heart before 'them' in 'their' presence. . . . 'For nothing in the world! never!' murmured Litvinov, inhaling deep draughts of the fresh air and descending the road towards Baden almost at a run. He thought of his betrothed, his sweet, good, sacred Tatyana, and how pure, how noble, how true she seemed to him. With what unmixed tenderness he recalled her features, her words, her very gestures . . . with what impatience he looked forward to her return.

The rapid exercise soothed his nerves. Returning home he sat down at the table and took up a book; suddenly he let it fall, even with a shudder. . . What had happened to him? Nothing had happened, but Irina . . . Irina. . . . All at once his meeting with her seemed something marvellous, strange, extraordinary. Was it possible? he had met, he had talked with the same Irina. . . . And why was there no trace in her of that hateful worldliness which was so sharply stamped upon all these others. Why did he fancy that she seemed, as it were, weary, or sad, or sick of her position? She was in their camp, but she was not an enemy. And what could have impelled her to receive him joyfully, to invite him to see her?

Litvinov started. 'O Tanya, Tanya!' he cried passionately, 'you are my guardian angel, you only, my good genius. I love you only and will love you for ever. And I will not go to see *her*. Forget her altogether! Let her amuse herself with her generals.' Litvinov set to his book again.

XI

LITVINOV took up his book again, but he could not read. He went out of the house, walked a little, listened to the music, glanced in at the gambling, returned again to his room, and tried again to read—still without success. The time seemed to drag by with peculiar dreariness. Pishtchalkin, the well-intentioned peaceable mediator, came in and sat with him for three hours. He talked, argued, stated questions, and discoursed intermittently, first of elevated, and then of practical topics, and succeeded in diffusing around him such an atmosphere of dulness that poor Litvinov was ready to cry. In raising dulness—agonising, chilling, helpless, hopeless dulness—to a fine art, Pishtchalkin was absolutely unrivalled even among persons of the highest morality, who are notoriously masters in that line. The mere sight of his well-cut and well-brushed head, his clear lifeless eyes, his benevolent nose, produced an involuntary despondency, and his deliberate, drowsy, lazy tone seemed to have been created only to state with conviction and lucidity such sententious truths as that twice two makes four and not five or three, that water is liquid, and benevolence laudable; that to the private individual, no less than to the state, and to the state no less than to the private individual, credit is absolutely indispensable for financial operations. And with all this he was such an excellent man! But such is the sentence the fates have passed on Russia; among us, good men are dull. Pishtchalkin retreated at last; he was replaced by Bindasov, who, without any beating about the bush, asked Litvinov with great effrontery for a loan of a hundred guldens, and the latter gave it him, in spite of the fact that Bindasov was not only unattractive, but even repulsive to him, that he knew for certain that he would never get his money back; and was, besides, himself in need of it. What made him give him the money then, the reader will inquire. Who can tell! That is another Russian weakness. Let the reader lay his hand on his heart and remember how many acts in his own life have had absolutely no other reason. And Bindasov did not even thank Litvinov; he asked for a glass of red Baden wine, and without wiping his lips departed, loudly and offensively tramping with his boots. And how vexed Litvinov was with himself already, as he watched the red nape of the retreating sharper's neck! Before evening he received a letter from Tatyana in which she informed him that as her aunt was not well, she could not come to Baden for five or six days. This news had a depressing influence on Litvinov; it increased his vexation, and he went to bed early in a disagreeable frame of mind. The following day turned out no better, if not worse, than the preceding. From early morning Litvinov's room was filled with his own countrymen; Bambaev, Voroshilov, Pishtchalkin, the two officers, the two Heidelberg students, all crowded in at once, and yet did not go away right up till dinner time, though they had soon said all they had to say and were obviously bored. They simply did not know what to do with themselves, and having got into Litvinov's lodgings they 'stuck' there, as they say. First they discussed the fact that Gubaryov had gone back to Heidelberg, and that they would have to go after him; then they philosophised a little, and touched on the Polish question; then they advanced to reflections on gambling and *cocottes*, and fell to repeating scandalous anecdotes; at last the conversation sank into a discussion of all sorts of 'strong men' and monsters of obesity and gluttony. First, they trotted out all the ancient stories of Lukin, of the deacon who ate no less than thirty-three herrings for a wager, of the Uhlan colonel, Ezyedinov, renowned for his corpulence, and of the soldier who broke the shin-bone on his own forehead; then followed unadulterated lying. Pishtchalkin himself related with a yawn that he knew a peasant woman in Little Russia, who at the time of her death had proved to weigh half a ton and some pounds, and a landowner who had eaten three geese and a sturgeon for luncheon; Bambaev suddenly fell into an ecstatic condition, and declared he himself was able to eat a whole sheep, 'with seasoning' of course; and Voroshilov burst out with something about a comrade, an athletic cadet, so grotesque that every one was reduced to silence, and after looking at each other, they took up their hats, and the party broke up. Litvinov, when he was left alone, tried to occupy himself, but he felt just as if his head was full of smouldering soot; he could do nothing that was of any use, and the evening too was wasted. The next morning he was just preparing for lunch, when some one knocked at his door. 'Good Lord,' thought Litvinov, 'one of yesterday's dear friends again,' and not without some trepidation he pronounced:

'*Herein!*'

The door opened slowly and in walked Potugin. Litvinov was exceedingly delighted to see him.

'This is nice!' he began, warmly shaking hands with his unexpected visitor, 'this is good of you! I should certainly have looked you up myself, but you would not tell me where you live. Sit down, please, put down your hat. Sit down.'

Potugin made no response to Litvinov's warm welcome, and remained standing in the middle of the room, shifting from one leg to the other; he only laughed a little and shook his head. Litvinov's cordial reception obviously touched him, but there was some constraint in the expression of his face.

'There's . . . some little misunderstanding,' he began, not without hesitation. 'Of course, it would always be . . . a pleasure . . . to me . . . but I have been sent . . . especially to you.'

'That's to say, do you mean,' commented Litvinov in an injured voice, 'that you would not have come to me of your own accord?'

'Oh, no, . . . indeed! But I . . . I should, perhaps, not have made up my mind to intrude on you to-day, if I had not been asked to come to you. In fact, I have a message for you.'

'From whom, may I ask?'

'From a person you know, from Irina Pavlovna Ratmirov. You promised three days ago to go and see her and you have not been.'

Litvinov stared at Potugin in amazement.

'You know Madame Ratmirov?'

'As you see.'

'And you know her well?'

'I am to a certain degree a friend of hers.'

Litvinov was silent for a little.

'Allow me to ask you,' he began at last, 'do you know why Irina Pavlovna wants to see me?'

Potugin went up to the window.

'To a certain degree I do. She was, as far as I can judge, very pleased at meeting you,—well,—and she wants to renew your former relations.'

'Renew,' repeated Litvinov. 'Excuse my indiscretion, but allow me to question you a little more. Do you know what was the nature of those relations?'

'Strictly speaking ... no, I don't know. But I imagine,' added Potugin, turning suddenly to Litvinov and looking affectionately at him, 'I imagine that they were of some value. Irina Pavlovna spoke very highly of you, and I was obliged to promise her I would bring you. Will you come?'

'When?'

'Now . . . at once.'

Litvinov merely made a gesture with his hand.

'Irina Pavlovna,' pursued Potugin, 'supposes that the . . . how can I express it . . . the environment, shall we say, in which you found her the other day, was not likely to be particularly attractive to you; but she told me to tell you, that the devil is not so black as he is fancied.'

'Hm. . . . Does that saying apply strictly to the environment?'

'Yes . . . and in general.'

'Hm. . . . Well, and what is your opinion, Sozont Ivanitch, of the devil?'

'I think, Grigory Mihalitch, that he is in any case not what he is fancied.'

'Is he better?'

'Whether better or worse it's hard to say, but certainly he is not the same as he is fancied. Well, shall we go?'

'Sit here a little first. I must own that it still seems rather strange to me.'

'What seems strange, may I make bold to inquire?'

'In what way can you have become a friend of Irina Pavlovna?'

Potugin scanned himself.

'With my appearance, and my position in

society, it certainly does seem rather incredible; but you know—Shakespeare has said already, "There are more things in heaven and earth, Horatio, etc." Life too is not to be trifled with. Here is a simile for you; a tree stands before you when there is no wind; in what way can a leaf on a lower branch touch a leaf on an upper branch? It's impossible. But when the storm rises it is all changed . . . and the two leaves touch.'

'Aha! So there were storms?'

'I should think so! Can one live without them? But enough of philosophy. It's time to go.'

Litvinov was still hesitating.

'O good Lord!' cried Potugin with a comic face, 'what are young men coming to nowadays! A most charming lady invites them to see her, sends messengers after them on purpose, and they raise difficulties. You ought to be ashamed, my dear sir, you ought to be ashamed. Here's your hat. Take it and "Vorwärts," as our ardent friends the Germans say.'

Litvinov still stood irresolute for a moment, but he ended by taking his hat and going out of the room with Potugin.

XII

THEY went to one of the best hotels in Baden and asked for Madame Ratmirov. The porter first inquired their names, and then answered at once that '*die Frau Fürstin ist zu Hause*,' and went himself to conduct them up the staircase and knock at the door of the apartment and announce them. '*Die Frau Fürstin*' received them promptly: she was alone, her husband had gone off to Carlsruhe for an interview with a great official, an influential personage who was passing through that town.

Irina was sitting at a small table, embroidering on canvas when Potugin and Litvinov crossed the threshold. She quickly flung her embroidery aside, pushed away the little table and got up; an expression of genuine pleasure overspread her face. She wore a morning dress, high at the neck; the superb lines of her shoulders and arms could be seen through the thin stuff; her carelessly-coiled hair had come loose and fell low on her slender neck. Irina flung a swift glance at Potugin, murmured '*merci*,' and holding out her hand to Litvinov reproached him amicably for forgetfulness.

'And you such an old friend!' she added.

Litvinov was beginning to apologise. '*C'est bien, c'est bien*,' she assented hurriedly and, taking his hat from him, with friendly insistence made him sit down. Potugin, too, was sitting down, but got up again directly, and saying that he had an engagement he could not put off, and that he would come in again after dinner, he proceeded to take leave. Irina again flung him a rapid glance, and gave him a friendly nod, but she did not try to keep him, and directly he had vanished behind the portière, she turned with eager impatience to Litvinov.

'Grigory Mihalitch,' she began, speaking Russian in her soft musical voice, 'here we are alone at last, and I can tell you how glad I am at our meeting, because it . . . it gives me a chance . . .' (Irina looked him straight in the face) 'of asking your forgiveness.'

Litvinov gave an involuntary start. He had not expected so swift an attack. He had not expected she would herself turn the conversation upon old times.

'Forgiveness . . . for what?' . . . he muttered.

Irina flushed.

'For what? . . . you know for what,' she said, and she turned slightly away. 'I wronged you, Grigory Mihalitch . . . though, of course, it was my fate' (Litvinov was reminded of her letter) 'and I do not regret it . . . it would be in any case too late; but, meeting you so unexpectedly, I said to myself that we absolutely must become friends, absolutely . . . and I should feel it deeply, if it did not come about . . . and it seems to me for that we must have an explanation, without putting it off, and once for all, so that afterwards there should be no . . . *gêne*, no awkwardness, once for all, Grigory Mihalitch; and that you must tell me you forgive me, or else I shall imagine you feel . . . *de la rancune*. *Voilà!* It is perhaps a great piece of fatuity on my part, for you have probably forgotten everything long, long ago, but no matter, tell me, you have forgiven me.'

Irina uttered this whole speech without taking breath, and Litvinov could see that there were tears shining in her eyes . . . yes, actually tears.

'Really, Irina Pavlovna,' he began hurriedly, 'how can you beg my pardon, ask forgiveness? . . . That is all past and buried, and I can only feel astounded that, in the midst of all the splendour which surrounds you, you have still preserved a recollection of the obscure companions of your youth. . . .'

'Does it astound you?' said Irina softly.

'It touches me,' Litvinov went on, 'because I could never have imagined——'

'You have not told me you have forgiven me, though,' interposed Irina.

'I sincerely rejoice at your happiness, Irina Pavlovna. With my whole heart I wish you all that is best on earth. . . .'

'And you will not remember evil against me?'

I will remember nothing but the happy moments for which I was once indebted to you.'

Irina held out both hands to him; Litvinov clasped them warmly, and did not at once let them go. . . . Something that long had not been, secretly stirred in his heart at that soft contact. Irina was again looking straight into his face; but this time she was smiling. . . . And he for the first time gazed directly and intently at her. . . . Again he recognised the features once so precious, and those deep eyes, with their marvellous lashes, and the little mole on her cheek, and the peculiar growth of her hair on her forehead, and her habit of somehow sweetly and humorously curving her lips and faintly twitching her eyebrows, all, all he recognised. . . . But how beautiful she had grown! What fascination, what power in her fresh, woman's body! And no rouge, no touching up, no powder, nothing false on that fresh pure face... Yes, this was a beautiful woman. A mood of musing came upon Litvinov.... He was still looking at her, but his thoughts were far away.... Irina perceived it.

'Well, that is excellent,' she said aloud; 'now my conscience is at rest then, and I can satisfy my curiosity.'

'Curiosity,' repeated Litvinov, as though puzzled.

'Yes, yes.... I want above all things to know what you have been doing all this time, what plans you have; I want to know all, how, what, when ... all, all. And you will have to tell me the truth, for I must warn you, I have not lost sight of you ... so far as I could.'

'You did not lose sight of me, you ... there ... in Petersburg?'

'In the midst of the splendour which surrounded me, as you expressed it just now. Positively, yes, I did not. As for that splendour we will talk about that again; but now you must tell me, you must tell me so much, at such length, no one will disturb us. Ah, how delightful it will be,' added Irina, gaily sitting down and arranging herself at her ease in an armchair. 'Come, begin.'

'Before telling my story, I have to thank you,' began Litvinov.

'What for?'

'For the bouquet of flowers, which made its appearance in my room.'

'What bouquet? I know nothing about it.'

'What?'

'I tell you I know nothing about it. . . . But I am waiting. . . I am waiting for your story. . . . Ah, what a good fellow that Potugin is to have brought you!'

Litvinov pricked up his ears.

'Have you known this Mr. Potugin long?' he queried.

'Yes, a long while . . . but tell me your story.'

'And do you know him well?'

'Oh, yes!' Irina sighed. 'There are special reasons. . . . You have heard, of course, of Eliza Byelsky. . . . Who died, you know, the year before last, such a dreadful death? . . Ah, to be sure, I'd forgotten you don't know all our scandals. . . . It is well, it is well indeed, that you don't know them. *O quelle chance!* at last, at last, a man, a live man, who knows nothing of us! And to be able to talk Russian with him, bad Russian of course, but still Russian, not that everlasting mawkish, sickening French patter of Petersburg.'

'And Potugin, you say, was connected with—'

'It's very painful for me even to refer to it,' Irina broke in. 'Eliza was my greatest friend at school, and afterwards in Petersburg we saw each other continually. She confided all her secrets to me, she was very unhappy, she suffered much. Potugin behaved splendidly in the affair, with true chivalry. He sacrificed himself. It was only then I learnt to appreciate him! But we have drifted away again. I am waiting for your story, Grigory Mihalitch.'

'But my story cannot interest you the least, Irina Pavlovna.'

'That's not your affair.'

'Think, Irina Pavlovna, we have not seen each other for ten years, ten whole years. How much water has flowed by since then.'

'Not water only! not water only!' she repeated with a peculiar bitter expression; 'that's just why I want to hear what you are going to tell me.'

'And beside I really don't know where to begin.'

'At the beginning. From the very time when you . . . when I went away to Petersburg. You left Moscow then. . . . Do you know I have never been back to Moscow since!'

'Really?'

'It was impossible at first; and afterwards when I was married——.'

'Have you been married long?'

'Four years.'

'Have you no children?'

'No,' she answered drily.

Litvinov was silent for a little.

'And did you go on living at that, what was his name, Count Reisenbach's, till your marriage?'

Irina looked steadily at him, as though she were trying to make up her mind why he asked that question.

'No,' . . . was her answer at last.

'I suppose, your parents. . . . By the way, haven't asked after them. Are they——'

'They are both well.'

'And living at Moscow as before?'

'At Moscow as before.'

'And your brothers and sisters?'

'They are all right; I have provided for all of them.'

'Ah!' Litvinov glanced up from under his brows at Irina. 'In reality, Irina Pavlovna, it's not I who ought to tell my story, but you, if only——' He suddenly felt embarrassed and stopped.

Irina raised her hands to her face and turned her wedding-ring round upon her finger.

'Well? I will not refuse,' she assented at last. 'Some day . . . perhaps. . . But first you . . . because, do you see, though I tried to follow you up, I know scarcely anything of you; while of me . . . well, of me you have heard enough certainly. Haven't you? I suppose you have heard of me, tell me?'

'You, Irina Pavlovna, occupied too conspicuous a place in the world, not to be the subject of talk . . . especially in the provinces, where I have been and where every rumour is believed.'

'And do you believe the rumours? And of what kind were the rumours?'

'To tell the truth, Irina Pavlovna, such rumours very seldom reached me. I have led a very solitary life.'

'How so? why, you were in the Crimea, in the militia?'

'You know that too?'

'As you see. I tell you, you have been watched.'

Again Litvinov felt puzzled.

'Why am I to tell you what you know without me?' said Litvinov in an undertone.

'Why . . . to do what I ask you. You see I ask you, Grigory Mihalitch.'

Litvinov bowed his head and began . . began in rather a confused fashion to recount in rough outline to Irina his uninteresting adventures. He often stopped and looked inquiringly at Irina, as though to ask whether he had told enough. But she insistently demanded the continuation of his narrative and pushing her hair back behind her ears, her elbows on the arm of her chair, she seemed to be catching every word with strained attention. Looking at her from one side and following the expression on her face, any one might perhaps have imagined she did not hear what Litvinov was saying at all, but was only deep in meditation. . But it was not of Litvinov she was meditating, though he grew confused and red under her persistent gaze. A whole life was rising up before her, a very different one, not his life, but her own.

Litvinov did not finish his story, but stopped short under the influence of an unpleasant sense of growing inner discomfort. This time Irina said nothing to him, and did not urge him to go on, but pressing her open hand to her eyes, as though she were tired, she leaned slowly back in her chair, and remained motionless. Litvinov waited for a little; then, reflecting that his visit had already lasted more than two hours, he was stretching out his hand for his hat, when suddenly in an adjoining room there was the sound of the rapid creak of thin kid boots, and preceded by the same exquisite aristocratic perfume, there entered Valerian Vladimirovitch Ratmirov.

Litvinov rose and interchanged bows with the good-looking general, while Irina, with no sign of haste, took her hand from her face, and looking coldly at her husband, remarked in French, 'Ah! so you've come back! But what time is it?'

'Nearly four, *ma chère amie*, and you not dressed yet—the princess will be expecting us,' answered the general; and with an elegant bend of his tightly-laced figure in Litvinov's direction, he added with the almost effeminate playfulness of intonation characteristic of him, 'It's clear an agreeable visitor has made you forgetful of time.'

The reader will permit us at this point to give him some information about General Ratmirov. His father was the natural . . . what do you suppose? You are not wrong—but we didn't mean to say that . . . the natural son of an illustrious personage of the reign of Alexander I. and of a pretty little French actress. The illustrious personage brought his son forward in the world, but left him no fortune, and the son himself (the father of our hero) had not time to grow rich; he died before he had risen above the rank of a colonel in the police. A year before his death he had married a handsome young widow who had happened to put herself under his protection. His son by the widow, Valerian Alexandrovitch, having got into the Corps of Pages by favour, attracted the notice of the authorities, not so much by his success in the sciences, as by his fine bearing, his fine manners, and his good behaviour (though he had been exposed to all that pupils in the government military schools were inevitably exposed to in former days) and went into the Guards. His career was a brilliant one, thanks to the discreet gaiety of his disposition, his skill in dancing, his excellent seat on horseback when an orderly at reviews, and lastly, by a kind of special trick of deferential familiarity with his superiors, of tender, attentive almost clinging subservience, with a flavour of vague liberalism, light as air. . . . This liberalism had not, however, prevented him from flogging fifty peasants in a White Russian village, where he had been sent to put down a riot. His personal appearance was most prepossessing and singularly youthful-looking; smooth-faced and rosy-cheeked, pliant and persistent, he made the most of his amazing success with women; ladies of the highest rank and mature age simply went out of their senses over him. Cautious from habit, silent from motives of prudence, General Ratmirov moved constantly in the highest society, like the busy bee gathering honey even from the least attractive flowers—and without morals, without information of any kind, but with the reputation of being good at business; with an insight into men, and a ready comprehension of the exigencies of the moment, and above all, a never-swerving desire for his own advantage, he saw at last all paths lying open before him. . . .

Litvinov smiled constrainedly, while Irina merely shrugged her shoulders.

'Well,' she said in the same cold tone, 'did you see the Count?'

'To be sure I saw him. He told me to remember him to you.'

'Ah! is he as imbecile as ever, that patron of yours?'

General Ratmirov made no reply. He only smiled to himself, as though lenient to the overhastiness of a woman's judgment. With just such a smile kindly-disposed grown-up people respond to the nonsensical whims of children.

'Yes,' Irina went on, 'the stupidity of your friend the Count is too striking, even when one has seen a good deal of the world.'

'You sent me to him yourself,' muttered the general, and turning to Litvinov he asked him in Russian, 'Was he getting any benefit from the Baden waters?'

'I am in perfect health, I'm thankful to say,' answered Litvinov.

'That's the greatest of blessings,' pursued the general, with an affable grimace; 'and indeed one doesn't, as a rule, come to Baden for the waters; but the waters here are very effectual, *je veux dire, efficaces*; and any one who suffers, as I do for instance, from a nervous cough——'

Irina rose quickly. 'We will see each other again, Grigory Mihalitch, and I hope soon,' she said in French, contemptuously cutting short her husband's speech, 'but now I must go and dress. That old princess is insufferable with her everlasting *parties de plaisir*, of which nothing comes but boredom.'

'You're hard on every one to-day,' muttered her husband, and he slipped away into the next room.

Litvinov was turning towards the door. . . . Irina stopped him.

'You have told me everything,' she said, 'but the chief thing you concealed.'

'What's that?'

'You are going to be married, I'm told?'

Litvinov blushed up to his ears. . . . As a fact, he had intentionally not referred to Tanya; but he felt horribly vexed, first, that Irina knew about his marriage, and, secondly, that she had, as it were, convicted him of a desire to conceal it from her. He was completely at a loss what to say, while Irina did not take her eyes off him.

'Yes, I am going to be married,' he said at last, and at once withdrew.

Ratmirov came back into the room.

'Well, why aren't you dressed?' he asked.

'You can go alone; my head aches.'

'But the princess . . .'

Irina scanned her husband from head to foot in one look, turned her back upon him, and went away to her boudoir.

XIII

LITVINOV felt much annoyed with himself, as though he had lost money at roulette, or failed to keep his word. An inward voice told him that he—on the eve of marriage, a man of sober sense, not a boy—ought not to have given way to the promptings of curiosity, nor the allurements of recollection. 'Much need there was to go!' he reflected. 'On her side simply flirtation, whim, caprice. . . . She's bored, she's sick of everything, she clutched at me . . . as some one pampered with dainties will suddenly long for black bread . . . well, that's natural enough. . . . But why did I go? Can I feel anything but contempt for her?' This last phrase he could not utter even in thought without an effort. . . . 'Of course, there's no kind of danger, and never could be,' he pursued his reflections. 'I know whom I have to deal with. But still one ought not to play with fire. . . . I'll never set my foot in her place again.' Litvinov dared not, or could not as yet, confess to himself how beautiful Irina had seemed to him, how powerfully she had worked upon his feelings.

Again the day passed dully and drearily. At dinner, Litvinov chanced to sit beside a majestic *belhomme*, with dyed moustaches, who said nothing, and only panted and rolled his eyes . . . but, being suddenly taken with a hiccup, proved himself to be a fellow-countryman, by at once exclaiming, with feeling, in Russian, 'There, I said I ought not to eat melons!' In the evening, too, nothing happened to compensate for a lost day; Bindasov, before Litvinov's very eyes, won a sum four times what he had borrowed from him, but, far from repaying his debt, he positively glared in his face with a menacing air, as though he were prepared to borrow more from him just because he had been a witness of his winnings. The next morning he was again invaded by a host of his compatriots; Litvinov got rid of them with difficulty, and setting off to the mountains, he first came across Irina—he pretended not to recognise her, and passed quickly by—and then Potugin. He was about to begin a conversation with Potugin, but the latter did not respond to him readily. He was leading by the hand a smartly dressed little girl, with fluffy, almost white curls, large black eyes, and a pale, sickly little face, with that peculiar peremptory and impatient expression characteristic of spoiled children. Litvinov spent two hours in the mountains, and then went back homewards along the Lichtenthaler Allee. . . . A lady, sitting on a bench, with a blue veil over her face, got up quickly, and came up to him. . . . He recognised Irina.

'Why do you avoid me, Grigory Mihalitch?' she said, in the unsteady voice of one who is boiling over within.

Litvinov was taken aback. 'I avoid you, Irina Pavlovna?'

'Yes, you . . . you——'

Irina seemed excited, almost angry.

'You are mistaken, I assure you.'

'No, I am not mistaken. Do you suppose this morning—when we met, I mean—do you suppose I didn't see that you knew me? Do you mean to say you did not know me? Tell me.'

'I really . . . Irina Pavlovna——

'Grigory Mihalitch, you're a straightforward man, you have always told the truth; tell me, tell me, you knew me, didn't you? you turned away on purpose?'

Litvinov glanced at Irina. Her eyes shone with a strange light, while her cheeks and lips were of a deathly pallor under the thick net of her veil. In the expression of her face, in the very sound of her abruptly jerked-out whisper, there was something so irresistibly mournful, beseeching . . . Litvinov could not pretend any longer.

'Yes . . . I knew you,' he uttered not without effort.

Irina slowly shuddered, and slowly dropped her hands.

'Why did you not come up to me?' she whispered.

'Why . . . why!' Litvinov moved on one side, away from the path, Irina followed him in silence. 'Why?' he repeated once more, and suddenly his face was aflame, and he felt his chest and throat choking with a passion akin to hatred. 'You . . . you ask such a question, after all that has passed between us? Not now, of course, not now; but there . . . there . . in Moscow.'

'But, you know, we decided; you know, you promised——' Irina was beginning.

'I have promised nothing! Pardon the harshness of my expressions, but you ask for the truth—so think for yourself: to what but a caprice—incomprehensible, I confess, to me—to what but a desire to try how much power you still have over me, can I attribute your . . . I don't know what to call it . . . your persistence? Our paths have lain so far apart! I have forgotten it all, I've lived through all that suffering long ago, I've become a different man completely; you are married—happy, at least, in appearance—you fill an envied position in the world; what's the object, what's the use of our meeting? What am I to you? what are you to me? We cannot even understand each other now; there is absolutely nothing in common between us now, neither in the past nor in the present! Especially . . . especially in the past!'

Litvinov uttered all this speech hurriedly, jerkily, without turning his head. Irina did not stir, except from time to time she faintly stretched her hands out to him. It seemed as though she were beseeching him to stop and listen to her, while, at his last words, she slightly bit her lower lip, as though to master the pain of a sharp, rapid wound.

'Grigory Mihalitch,' she began at last, in a calmer voice; and she moved still further away from the path, along which people from time to time passed.

Litvinov in his turn followed her.

'Grigory Mihalitch, believe me, if I could imagine I had one hair's-breadth of power over you left, I would be the first to avoid you. If I have not done so, if I made up my mind, in spite of my . . . of the wrong I did you in the past, to renew my acquaintance with you, it was because . . . because——'

'Because what?' asked Litvinov, almost rudely.

'Because,' Irina declared with sudden force—'it's too insufferable, too unbearably stifling for me in society, in the envied position you talk about; because meeting you, a live man, after all these dead puppets—you have seen samples of them three days ago, there *au Vieux Château*,—I rejoice over you as an oasis in the desert, while you suspect me of flirting, and despise me and repulse me on the ground that I wronged you—as indeed I did—but far more myself!'

'You chose your lot yourself, Irina Pavlovna, Litvinov rejoined sullenly, as before not turning his head.

'I chose it myself, yes . . . and I don't complain, I have no right to complain,' said Irina hurriedly; she seemed to derive a secret consolation from Litvinov's very harshness. 'I know that you must think ill of me, and I won't justify myself; I only want to explain my feeling to you, I want to convince you I am in no flirting humour now. . . . Me flirting with you! Why, there is no sense in it. . . . When I saw you, all that was good, that was young in me, revived . . . that time when I had not yet chosen my lot, everything that lies behind in that streak of brightness behind those ten years. . . .'

'Come, really, Irina Pavlovna! So far as I am aware, the brightness in your life began precisely with the time we separated. . . .'

Irina put her handkerchief to her lips.

'That's very cruel, what you say, Grigory Mihalitch; but I can't feel angry with you. Oh, no, that was not a bright time, it was not for happiness I left Moscow; I have known not one moment, not one instant of happiness . . . believe me, whatever you have been told. If I were happy, could I talk to you as I am talking now. . . . I repeat to you, you don't know what these people are. . . . Why, they understand nothing, feel for nothing; they've no intelligence even, *ni esprit ni intelligence*, nothing but tact and cunning; why, in reality, music and poetry and art are all equally remote from them. . . . You will say that I was rather indifferent to all that myself; but not to the same degree, Grigory Mihalitch . . . not to the same degree! It's not a woman of the world before you now, you need only look at me—not a society queen. . . . That's what they call us, I believe . . . but a poor, poor creature, really deserving of pity. Don't wonder at my words.

'... I am beyond feeling pride now! I hold out my hand to you as a beggar, will you understand, just as a beggar. ... I ask for charity,' she added suddenly, in an involuntary, irrepressible outburst, 'I ask for charity, and you——'

Her voice broke. Litvinov raised his head and looked at Irina; her breathing came quickly, her lips were quivering. Suddenly his heart beat fast, and the feeling of hatred vanished.

'You say that our paths have lain apart,' Irina went on. 'I know you are about to marry from inclination, you have a plan laid out for your whole life; yes, that's all so, but we have not become strangers to one another, Grigory Mihalitch; we can still understand each other. Or do you imagine I have grown altogether dull—altogether debased in the mire? Ah, no, don't think that, please! Let me open my heart, I beseech you—there—even for the sake of those old days, if you are not willing to forget them. Do so, that our meeting may not have come to pass in vain; that would be too bitter; it would not last long in any case. ... I don't know how to say it properly, but you will understand me, because I ask for little, so little ... only a little sympathy, only that you should not repulse me, that you should let me open my heart——'

Irina ceased speaking, there were tears in her voice. She sighed, and timidly, with a kind of furtive, searching look, gazed at Litvinov, held out her hand to him...

Litvinov slowly took the hand and faintly pressed it.

'Let us be friends,' whispered Irina.

'Friends,' repeated Litvinov dreamily.

'Yes, friends . . . or if that is too much to ask, then let us at least be friendly. . . . Let us be simply as though nothing had happened.'

'As though nothing had happened, . . .' repeated Litvinov again. 'You said just now, Irina Pavlovna, that I was unwilling to forget the old days. . . . But what if I can't forget them?'

A blissful smile flashed over Irina's face, and at once disappeared, to be replaced by a harassed, almost scared expression.

'Be like me, Grigory Mihalitch, remember only what was good in them; and most of all, give me your word. . . . Your word of honour. . . .'

'Well?'

'Not to avoid me . . . not to hurt me for nothing. You promise? tell me!'

'Yes.'

'And you will dismiss all evil thoughts of me from your mind.'

'Yes . . . but as for understanding you—I give it up.'

'There's no need of that . . . wait a little, though, you will understand. But you will promise?'

'I have said yes already.'

'Thanks. You see I am used to believe you. I shall expect you to-day, to-morrow, I will not go out of the house. And now I must leave you. The Grand Duchess is coming along the avenue. . . . She's caught sight of me, and I can't avoid going up to speak to her. . . . Good-bye till we meet. . . . Give me your hand, *vite, vite*. Till we meet.'

And warmly pressing Litvinov's hand, Irina walked towards a middle-aged person of dignified appearance, who was coming slowly along the gravel path, escorted by two other ladies, and a strikingly handsome groom in livery.

'*Eh bonjour, chère Madame,*' said the personage, while Irina curtseyed respectfully to her. '*Comment allez-vous aujourd'hui? Venez un peu avec moi.*'

'*Votre Altesse a trop de bonté,*' Irina's insinuating voice was heard in reply.

XIV

LITVINOV let the Grand Duchess and all her suite get out of sight, and then he too went along the avenue. He could not make up his mind clearly what he was feeling; he was conscious both of shame and dread, while his vanity was flattered. . . . The unexpected explanation with Irina had taken him utterly by surprise; her rapid burning words had passed over him like a thunder-storm. 'Queer creatures these society women,' he thought; 'there's no consistency in them . . . and how perverted they are by the surroundings in which they go on living, while they're conscious of its hideousness themselves!' . . . In reality he was not thinking this at all, but only mechanically repeating these hackneyed phrases, as though he were trying to ward off other more painful thoughts. He felt that he must not think seriously just now, that he would probably have to blame himself, and he moved with lagging steps, almost forcing himself to pay attention to

everything that happened to meet him. . . .
He suddenly found himself before a seat, caught
sight of some one's legs in front of it, and looked
upwards from them. . . . The legs belonged to
a man, sitting on the seat, and reading a newspaper; this man turned out to be Potugin.
Litvinov uttered a faint exclamation. Potugin
laid the paper down on his knees, and looked
attentively, without a smile, at Litvinov; and
Litvinov also attentively, and also without a
smile, looked at Potugin.

'May I sit by you?' he asked at last.

'By all means, I shall be delighted. Only I
warn you, if you want to have a talk with me,
you mustn't be offended with me—I'm in a
most misanthropic humour just now, and I see
everything in an exaggeratedly repulsive light.'

'That's no matter, Sozont Ivanitch,' responded Litvinov, sinking down on the seat,
'indeed it's particularly appropriate. . . . But
why has such a mood come over you?'

'I ought not by rights to be ill-humoured,'
began Potugin. 'I've just read in the paper
a project for judicial reforms in Russia, and
I see with genuine pleasure that we've got
some sense at last, and they're not as usual
on the pretext of independence, nationalism,
or originality, proposing to tack a little
home-made tag of our own on to the clear

straightforward logic of Europe; but are taking what's good from abroad intact. A single adaptation in its application to the peasants' sphere is enough. . . . There's no doing away with communal ownership! . . . Certainly, certainly, I ought not to be ill-humoured; but to my misfortune I chanced upon a Russian "rough diamond," and had a talk with him, and these rough diamonds, these self-educated geniuses, would make me turn in my grave!'

'What do you mean by a rough diamond?' asked Litvinov.

'Why, there's a gentleman disporting himself here, who imagines he's a musical genius. "I have done nothing, of course," he'll tell you. "I'm a cipher, because I've had no training, but I've incomparably more melody and more ideas in me than in Meyerbeer." In the first place, I say: why have you had no training? and secondly, that, not to talk of Meyerbeer, the humblest German flute-player, modestly blowing his part in the humblest German orchestra, has twenty times as many ideas as all our untaught geniuses; only the flute-player keeps his ideas to himself, and doesn't trot them out with a flourish in the land of Mozarts and Haydns; while our friend the rough diamond has only to strum some little waltz or song, and at once you see him with his hands in his trouser pocket and a sneer of contempt on his lips: I'm a genius, he says. And in painting it's just the same, and in everything else. Oh, these natural geniuses, how I hate them! As if every one didn't know that it's only where there's no real science fully assimilated, and no real art, that there's this flaunting affectation of them. Surely it's time to have done with this flaunting, this vulgar twaddle, together with all hackneyed phrases such as "no one ever dies of hunger in Russia," "nowhere is there such fast travelling as in Russia," "we Russians could bury all our enemies under our hats." I'm for ever hearing of the richness of the Russian nature, their unerring instinct, and of Kulibin.... But what is this richness, after all, gentlemen? Half-awakened mutterings or else half-animal sagacity. Instinct, indeed! A fine boast. Take an ant in a forest and set it down a mile from its ant-hill, it will find its way home; man can do nothing like it; but what of it? do you suppose he's inferior to the ant? Instinct, be it ever so unerring, is unworthy of man; sense, simple, straightforward, common sense—that's our heritage, our pride; sense won't perform any such tricks, but it's that that everything rests upon. As for Kulibin, who without any knowledge of mechanics succeeded in making some very bad watches, why, I'd have those watches set up in the pillory, and say: see, good people, this is the way *not* to do it. Kulibin's not to blame for it, but his work's rubbish. To admire Telushkin's boldness and cleverness because he climbed on to the Admiralty spire is well enough; why not admire him? But there's no need to shout that he's made the German architects look foolish, that they're no good, except at making money. . . . He's not made them look foolish in the least; they had to put a scaffolding round the spire afterwards, and repair it in the usual way. For mercy's sake, never encourage the idea in Russia that anything can be done without training. No; you may have the brain of a Solomon, but you must study, study from the A B C. Or else hold your tongue, and sit still, and be humble! Phoo! it makes one hot all over!'

Potugin took off his hat and began fanning himself with his handkerchief.

'Russian art,' he began again. 'Russian art, indeed! . . . Russian impudence and conceit, I know, and Russian feebleness too, but Russian art, begging your pardon, I've never come across. For twenty years on end they've been doing homage to that bloated nonentity Bryullov, and fancying that we have founded a school of our own, and even that it will be better than all others... Russian art, ha, ha, ha! ho, ho!'

'Excuse me, though, Sozont Ivanitch,' remarked Litvinov, 'would you refuse to recognise Glinka too, then?'

Potugin scratched his head.

'The exception, you know, only proves the rule, but even in that instance we could not dispense with bragging. If we'd said, for example, that Glinka was really a remarkable musician, who was only prevented by circumstances—outer and inner—from becoming the founder of the Russian opera, none would have disputed it; but no, that was too much to expect! They must at once raise him to the dignity of commander-in-chief, of grand-marshal, in the musical world, and disparage other nations while they were about it; they have nothing to compare with him, they declare, then quote you some marvellous home-bred genius whose compositions are nothing but a poor imitation of second-rate foreign composers, yes, second-rate ones, for they're the easiest to imitate. Nothing to compare with him? Oh, poor benighted barbarians, for whom standards in art are non-existent, and artists are something of the same species as the strong man Rappo: there's a foreign prodigy, they say, can lift fifteen stone in one hand, but our man can lift thirty! Nothing to compare with us, indeed! I will venture to tell you something I remember, and can't get out of my head. Last spring I visited the Crystal Palace near London; in that Palace, as you're aware, there's a sort of exhibition of everything that has been devised by the ingenuity of man—an encyclopædia of humanity one might call it. Well, I walked to and fro among the machines and implements and statues of great men; and all the while I thought, if it were decreed that some nation or other should disappear from the face of the earth, and with it everything that nation had invented, should disappear from the Crystal Palace, our dear mother, Holy Russia, could go and hide herself in the lower regions, without disarranging a single nail in the place: everything might remain undisturbed where it is; for even the *samovar*, the woven bast shoes, the yoke-bridle, and the knout—these are our famous products—were not invented by us. One could not carry out the same experiment on the Sandwich islanders; those islanders have made some peculiar canoes and javelins of their own; their absence would be noticed by visitors. It's a libel! it's too severe, you say perhaps. . . . But I say, first, I don't know how to roar like any sucking dove; and secondly, it's plain that it's not only the devil no one dares to look straight in the face, for no one dares to look straight at himself, and it's not only children who like being soothed to sleep. Our older inventions came to us from the East, our later ones we've borrowed, and half spoiled, from the West, while we still persist in talking about the independence of Russian art! Some bold spirits have even discovered an original Russian science; twice two makes four with us as elsewhere, but the result's obtained more ingeniously, it appears.'

'But wait a minute, Sozont Ivanitch,' cried Litvinov. 'Do wait a minute! You know we send something to the universal exhibitions, and doesn't Europe import something from us.'

'Yes, raw material, raw products. And note, my dear sir: this raw produce of ours is generally only good by virtue of other exceedingly bad conditions; our bristles, for instance, are large and strong, because our pigs are poor; our hides are stout and thick because our cows are thin; our tallow's rich because it's boiled down with half the flesh. . . . But why am I enlarging on that to you, though; you are a student of technology, to be sure, you must know all that better than I do. They talk to me of our inventive faculty! The inventive faculty of the Russians! Why our worthy farmers complain bitterly and suffer loss because there's no satisfactory machine for drying grain in existence, to save them from the necessity of putting their sheaves in ovens, as they did in the days of Rurik; these ovens are fearfully wasteful—just as our bast shoes and our Russian mats are,—and they are constantly getting on fire. The farmers complain, but still there's no sign of a drying-machine. And why is there none? Because the German farmer doesn't need them; he can thrash his wheat as it is, so he doesn't bother to invent one, and we . . . are not capable of doing it! Not capable—and that's all about it! Try as we may! From this day forward I declare whenever I come across one of those rough diamonds, these self-taught geniuses, I shall say: "Stop a minute, my worthy friend! Where's that drying-machine? let's have it!" But that's beyond them! Picking up some old cast-off shoe, dropped ages ago by St. Simon or Fourier, and sticking it on our heads and treating it as a sacred relic—that's what we're capable of; or scribbling an article on the historical and contemporary significance of the proletariat in the principal towns of France—that we can do too; but I tried once, asking a writer and political economist of that sort—rather like your friend, Mr Voroshilov—to mention twenty towns in France, and what do you think came of that? Why the economist in despair at last mentioned Mont-Fermeuil as one of the French towns, remembering it probably from some novel of Paul de Kock's. And that reminds me of the following anecdote. I was one day strolling through a wood with a dog and a gun——'

'Are you a sportsman then?' asked Litvinov.

'I shoot a little. I was making my way to a swamp in search of snipe; I'd been told of the swamp by other sportsmen. I saw sitting in a clearing before a hut a timber merchant's clerk, as fresh and smooth as a peeled nut, he was sitting there, smiling away—what at, I can't say. So I asked him: "Whereabouts was the swamp, and were there many snipe in it?" "To be sure, to be sure," he sang out promptly, and with an expression of face as though I'd given him a rouble; "the swamp's first-rate, I'm thankful to say; and as for all kinds of wild fowl,—my goodness, they're to be found there in wonderful plenty." I set off, but not only found no wild fowl, the swamp itself had been dry for a long time. Now tell me, please, why is the Russian a liar? Why does the political economist lie, and why the lie about the wild fowl too?'

Litvinov made no answer, but only sighed sympathetically.

'But turn the conversation with the same political economist,' pursued Potugin, 'on the most abstruse problems of social science, keeping to theory, without facts . . . !—he takes flight like a bird, a perfect eagle. I did once succeed, though, in catching one of those birds. I used a pretty snare, though an obvious one, as you shall see if you please. I was talking with one of our latter-day " new young men " about various questions, as they call them. Well, he got very hot, as they always do. Marriage among other things he attacked with really childish exasperation. I brought forward one argument after another . . . I might as well have talked to a stone wall! I saw I should never get round him like that. And then I had a happy thought! "Allow me to submit to you," I began,—one must always talk very respectfully to these " new young men "— " I am really surprised at you, my dear sir; you are studying natural science, and your attention has never up till now been caught by the fact that all carnivorous and predatory animals —wild beasts and birds—all who have to go out in search of prey, and to exert themselves to obtain animal food for themselves and their young . . . and I suppose you would include man in the category of such animals?" "Of course, I should," said the "new young man,"

"man is nothing but a carnivorous animal." "And predatory?" I added. "And predatory," he declared. "Well said," I observed. "Well, then I am surprised you've never noticed that such animals live in monogamy." The "new young man" started. "How so?" "Why, it is so. Think of the lion, the wolf, the fox, the vulture, the kite; and, indeed, would you condescend to suggest how they could do otherwise. It's hard work enough for the two together to get a living for their offspring." My "new young man" grew thoughtful. "Well," says he, "in that case the animal is not a rule for man." Thereupon I called him an idealist, and wasn't he hurt at that! He almost cried. I had to comfort him by promising not to tell of him to his friends. To deserve to be called an idealist is no laughing matter! The main point in which our latter-day young people are out in their reckoning is this. They fancy that the time for the old, obscure, underground work is over, that it was all very well for their old-fashioned fathers to burrow like moles, but that's too humiliating a part for us, we will take action in the light of day, we will take action . . . Poor darlings! why your children even won't take action; and don't you care to go back to burrowing, burrowing underground again in the old tracks?'

A brief silence followed.

'I am of opinion, my dear sir,' began Potugin again, 'that we are not only indebted to civilisation for science, art, and law, but that even the very feeling for beauty and poetry is developed and strengthened under the influence of the same civilisation, and that the so-called popular, simple, unconscious creation is twaddling and rubbishy. Even in Homer there are traces of a refined and varied civilisation; love itself is enriched by it. The Slavophils would cheerfully hang me for such a heresy, if they were not such chicken-hearted creatures; but I will stick up for my own ideas all the same; and however much they press Madame Kohanovsky and "The swarm of bees at rest" upon me,—I can't stand the odour of that *triple extrait de mougik Russe*, as I don't belong to the highest society, which finds it absolutely necessary to assure itself from time to time that it has not turned quite French, and for whose exclusive benefit this literature *en cuir de Russie* is manufactured. Try reading the raciest, most "popular" passages from the "Bees" to a common peasant—a real one; he'll think you're repeating him a new spell against fever or drunkenness. I repeat, without civilisation there's not even poetry. If you want to get a clear idea of the poetic ideal of the uncivilised

Russian, you should turn up our ballads, our legends. To say nothing of the fact that love is always presented as the result of witchcraft, of sorcery, and produced by some philtre, to say nothing of our so-called epic literature being the only one among all the European and Asiatic literatures—the only one, observe, which does not present any typical pair of lovers — unless you reckon Vanka-Tanka as such; and of the Holy Russian knight always beginning his acquaintance with his destined bride by beating her "most pitilessly" on her white body, because "the race of women is puffed up"! all that I pass over; but I should like to call your attention to the artistic form of the young hero, the *jeune premier*, as he was depicted by the imagination of the primitive, uncivilised Slav. Just fancy him a minute; the *jeune premier* enters; a cloak he has worked himself of sable, back-stitched along every seam, a sash of seven-fold silk girt close about his armpits, his fingers hidden away under his hanging sleevelets, the collar of his coat raised high above his head, from before, his rosy face no man can see, nor, from behind, his little white neck; his cap is on one ear, while on his feet are boots of morocco, with points as sharp as a cobbler's awl, and the heels peaked like nails. Round the points an egg can be rolled, and a sparrow can fly under the heels. And the young hero advances with that peculiar mincing gait by means of which our Alcibiades, Tchivilo Plenkovitch, produced such a striking, almost medical, effect on old women and young girls, the same gait which we see in our loose-limbed waiters, that cream, that flower of Russian dandyism, that *ne plus ultra* of Russian taste. This I maintain without joking; a sack-like gracefulness, that's an artistic ideal. What do you think, is it a fine type? Does it present many materials for painting, for sculpture? And the beauty who fascinates the young hero, whose "face is as red as the blood of the hare"? ... But I think you're not listening to me?'

Litvinov started. He had not, in fact, heard what Potugin was saying; he kept thinking, persistently thinking of Irina, of his last interview with her. . . .

'I beg your pardon, Sozont Ivanitch,' he began, 'but I'm going to attack you again with my former question about . . . about Madame Ratmirov.'

Potugin folded up his newspaper and put it in his pocket.

'You want to know again how I came to know her?'

'No, not exactly. I should like to hear your

opinion . . . on the part she played in Petersburg. What was that part, in reality?'

'I really don't know what to say to you, Grigory Mihalitch; I was brought into rather intimate terms with Madame Ratmirov . . . but quite accidentally, and not for long. I never got an insight into her world, and what took place in it remained unknown to me. There was some gossip before me, but as you know, it's not only in democratic circles that slander reigns supreme among us. Besides I was not inquisitive. I see though,' he added, after a short silence, 'she interests you.'

'Yes; we have twice talked together rather openly. I ask myself, though, is she sincere?'

Potugin looked down. 'When she is carried away by feeling, she is sincere, like all women of strong passions. Pride too, sometimes prevents her from lying.'

'Is she proud? I should rather have supposed she was capricious.'

'Proud as the devil; but that's no harm.'

'I fancy she sometimes exaggerates. . . .'

'That's nothing either, she's sincere all the same. Though after all, how can you expect truth? The best of those society women are rotten to the marrow of their bones.'

'But, Sozont Ivanitch, if you remember, you

called yourself her friend. Didn't you drag me almost by force to go and see her?'

'What of that? she asked me to get hold of you; and I thought, why not? And I really am her friend. She has her good qualities: she's very kind, that is to say, generous, that's to say she gives others what she has no sort of need of herself. But of course you must know her at least as well as I do.'

'I used to know Irina Pavlovna ten years ago; but since then——'

'Ah, Grigory Mihalitch, why do you say that? Do you suppose any one's character changes? Such as one is in one's cradle, such one is still in one's tomb. Or perhaps it is' (here Potugin bowed his head still lower) 'perhaps, you're afraid of falling into her clutches? that's certainly . . . But of course one is bound to fall into some woman's clutches.'

Litvinov gave a constrained laugh. 'You think so?'

'There's no escape. Man is weak, woman is strong, opportunity is all-powerful, to make up one's mind to a joyless life is hard, to forget oneself utterly is impossible . . . and on one side is beauty and sympathy and warmth and light,—how is one to resist it? Why, one runs like a child to its nurse. Ah, well, afterwards to be sure comes cold and darkness and emptiness ... in due course. And you end by being strange to everything, by losing comprehension of everything. At first you don't understand how love is possible; afterwards one won't understand how life is possible.'

Litvinov looked at Potugin, and it struck him that he had never yet met a man more lonely, more desolate ... more unhappy. This time he was not shy, he was not stiff; downcast and pale, his head on his breast, and his hands on his knees, he sat without moving, merely smiling his dejected smile. Litvinov felt sorry for the poor, embittered, eccentric creature.

'Irina Pavlovna mentioned among other things,' he began in a low voice, 'a very intimate friend of hers, whose name if I remember was Byelsky, or Dolsky. . . .'

Potugin raised his mournful eyes and looked at Litvinov.

'Ah!' he commented thickly. . . . 'She mentioned . . . well, what of it? It's time, though,' he added with a rather artificial yawn, 'for me to be getting home—to dinner. Good-bye.'

He jumped up from the seat and made off quickly before Litvinov had time to utter a word. . . . His compassion gave way to annoyance—annoyance with himself, be it understood. Want of consideration of any kind was foreign to his nature; he had wished to express his sympathy for Potugin, and it had resulted in something like a clumsy insinuation. With secret dissatisfaction in his heart, he went back to his hotel.

'Rotten to the marrow of her bones,' he thought a little later. . . . 'but proud as the devil! She, that woman who is almost on her knees to me, proud? proud and not capricious?'

Litvinov tried to drive Irina's image out of his head, but he did not succeed. For this very reason he did not think of his betrothed; he felt to-day this haunting image would not give up its place. He made up his mind to await without further anxiety the solution of all this 'strange business'; the solution could not be long in coming, and Litvinov had not the slightest doubt it would turn out to be most innocent and natural. So he fancied, but meanwhile he was not only haunted by Irina's image—every word she had uttered kept recurring in its turn to his memory.

The waiter brought him a note: it was from the same Irina:

'If you have nothing to do this evening, come to me; I shall not be alone; I shall have guests, and you will get a closer view of our set, our society. I want you very much to see something of them; I fancy they will show themselves in all their brilliance. You ought to know what sort of atmosphere I am breathing. Come; I shall be glad to see you, and you will not be bored. (Irina had spelt the Russian incorrectly here.) Prove to me that our explanation to-day has made any sort of misunderstanding between us impossible for ever.—Yours devotedly, I.'

Litvinov put on a frock coat and a white tie, and set off to Irina's. 'All this is of no importance,' he repeated mentally on the way, 'as for looking at *them* . . . why shouldn't I have a look at them? It will be curious.' A few days before, these very people had aroused a different sensation in him; they had aroused his indignation.

He walked with quickened steps, his cap pulled down over his eyes, and a constrained smile on his lips, while Bambaev, sitting before Weber's café, and pointing him out from a distance to Voroshilov and Pishtchalkin, cried excitedly: 'Do you see that man? He's a stone! he's a rock! he's a flint!!!'

XV

LITVINOV found rather many guests at Irina's. In a corner at a card-table were sitting three of the generals of the picnic: the stout one, the irascible one, and the condescending one. They were playing whist with dummy, and there is no word in the language of man to express the solemnity with which they dealt, took tricks, led clubs and led diamonds . . . there was no doubt about their being statesmen now! These gallant generals left to mere commoners, *aux bourgeois,* the little turns and phrases commonly used during play, and uttered only the most indispensable syllables; the stout general however permitted himself to jerk off between two deals: '*Ce satané as de pique!*' Among the visitors Litvinov recognised ladies who had been present at the picnic; but there were others there also whom he had not seen before. There was one so ancient that it seemed every instant as though she would fall to pieces: she shrugged her bare, gruesome, dingy grey shoulders, and, covering her mouth with her fan, leered languishingly with her absolutely death-like eyes upon Ratmirov; he paid her much attention; she was held in great honour in the highest society, as the last of the Maids of Honour of the Empress Catherine. At the window, dressed like a shepherdess, sat Countess S., 'the Queen of the Wasps,' surrounded by young men. Among them the celebrated millionaire and beau Finikov was conspicuous for his supercilious deportment, his absolutely flat skull, and his expression of soulless brutality, worthy of a Khan of Bucharia, or a Roman Heliogabalus. Another lady, also a countess, known by the pet name of *Lise*, was talking to a long-haired, fair, and pale spiritualistic medium. Beside them was standing a gentleman, also pale and long-haired, who kept laughing in a meaning way. This gentleman also believed in spiritualism, but added to that an interest in prophecy, and, on the basis of the Apocalypse and the Talmud, was in the habit of foretelling all kinds of marvellous events. Not a single one of these events had come to pass; but he was in no wise disturbed by that fact, and went on prophesying as before. At the piano, the musical genius had installed himself, the rough diamond, who had stirred Potugin to such indignation; he was striking chords with a careless hand, *d'une main distraite*, and kept staring vaguely about him. Irina was sitting on a sofa between Prince Kokó and Madame H., once a celebrated beauty and wit, who had long ago become a repulsive old crone, with the odour of sanctity and evaporated sinfulness about her. On catching sight of Litvinov, Irina blushed and got up, and when he went up to her, she pressed his hand warmly. She was wearing a dress of black crépon, relieved by a few inconspicuous gold ornaments; her shoulders were a dead white, while her face, pale too, under the momentary flood of crimson overspreading it, was breathing with the triumph of beauty, and not of beauty alone; a hidden, almost ironical happiness was shining in her half-closed eyes, and quivering about her lips and nostrils. . . .

Ratmirov approached Litvinov and after exchanging with him his customary civilities, unaccompanied however by his customary playfulness, he presented him to two or three ladies: the ancient ruin, the Queen of the Wasps, Countess Liza . . . they gave him a rather gracious reception. Litvinov did not belong to their set; but he was good-looking, extremely so, indeed, and the expressive features of his youthful face awakened their interest. Only he did not know how to fasten that interest upon himself; he was unaccustomed to society and was conscious of some embarrassment, added to which the stout general stared at him persistently. 'Aha! lubberly civilian! free-thinker!' that fixed heavy stare seemed to be saying: 'down on your knees to us; crawl to kiss our hands!' Irina came to Litvinov's aid. She managed so adroitly that he got into a corner near the door, a little behind her. As she addressed him, she had each time to turn round to him, and every time he admired the exquisite curve of her splendid neck, he drank in the subtle fragrance of her hair. An expression of gratitude, deep and calm, never left her face; he could not help seeing that gratitude and nothing else was what those smiles, those glances expressed, and he too was all aglow with the same emotion, and he felt shame, and delight and dread at once . . . and at the same time she seemed continually as though she would ask, 'Well? what do you think of them?' With special clearness Litvinov heard this unspoken question whenever any one of the party was guilty of some vulgar phrase or act, and that occurred more than once during the evening. Once she did not even conceal her feelings, and laughed aloud.

Countess Liza, a lady of superstitious bent, with an inclination for everything extraordinary, after discoursing to her heart's content with the spiritualist upon Home, turning tables, self-playing concertinas, and so on, wound up by asking him whether there were animals which could be influenced by mesmerism.

'There is one such animal any way,' Prince Kokó declared from some way off. 'You know Melvanovsky, don't you? They put him to sleep before me, and didn't he snore, he, he!'

'You are very naughty, *mon prince*; I am speaking of real animals, *je parle des bêtes.*'

'*Mais moi aussi, madame, je parle d'une bête....*'

'There are such,' put in the spiritualist; 'for instance—crabs; they are very nervous, and are easily thrown into a cataleptic state.'

The countess was astounded. 'What? Crabs! Really? Oh, that's awfully interesting! Now, that I should like to see, M'sieu Luzhin,' she added to a young man with a face as stony as a new doll's, and a stony collar (he prided himself on the fact that he had bedewed the aforesaid face and collar with the sprays of Niagara and the Nubian Nile, though he remembered nothing of all his travels, and cared for nothing but Russian puns...). 'M'sieu Luzhin, if you would be so good, do bring us a crab quick.'

M'sieu Luzhin smirked. 'Quick must it be, or quickly?' he queried.

The countess did not understand him. '*Mais oui*, a crab,' she repeated, '*une écrevisse.*'

'Eh? what is it? a crab? a crab?' the Countess S. broke in harshly. The absence of M. Verdier irritated her; she could not imagine why Irina had not invited that most fascinating of Frenchmen. The ancient ruin, who had long since ceased understanding anything—moreover she was completely deaf—only shook her head.

'*Oui, oui, vous allez voir.* M'sieu Luzhin, please. . . .'

The young traveller bowed, went out, and returned quickly. A waiter walked behind him, and grinning from ear to ear, carried in a dish, on which a large black crab was to be seen.

'*Voici, madame,*' cried Luzhin; 'now we can proceed to the operation on cancer. Ha, ha, ha!' (Russians are always the first to laugh at their own witticisms.)

'He, he, he!' Count Kokó did his duty condescendingly as a good patriot, and patron of all national products.

(We beg the reader not to be amazed and indignant; who can say confidently for himself that sitting in the stalls of the Alexander Theatre, and infected by its atmosphere, he has not applauded even worse puns?)

'*Merci, merci,*' said the countess. '*Allons, allons, Monsieur Fox, montrez nous ça.*'

The waiter put the dish down on a little round table. There was a slight movement among the guests; several heads were craned forward; only the generals at the card-table preserved the serene solemnity of their pose. The spiritualist ruffled up his hair, frowned, and, approaching the table, began waving his hands in the air; the crab stretched itself, backed, and raised its claws. The spiritualist repeated and quickened his movements; the crab stretched itself as before.

'*Mais que doit-elle donc faire?*' inquired the countess.

'*Elle doâ rester immobile et se dresser sur sa quiou,*' replied Mr. Fox, with a strong American accent, and he brandished his fingers with convulsive energy over the dish; but the mesmerism had no effect, the crab continued to move. The spiritualist declared that he was not himself, and retired with an air of displeasure from the table. The countess began to console him, by assuring him that similar failures occurred sometimes even with Mr. Home. . . Prince Kokó confirmed her words. The authority on the Apocalypse and the Talmud stealthily went up to the table, and making rapid but vigorous thrusts with his fingers in the direction of the crab, he too tried his luck, but without success; no symptom of catalepsy showed itself. Then the waiter was called, and told to take away the crab, which he accordingly did, grinning from ear to ear, as before; he could be heard exploding outside the door. . . . There was much laughter afterwards in the kitchen *über diese Russen.* The self-taught genius, who had gone on striking notes during the experiments with the crab, dwelling on melancholy chords, on the ground that there was no knowing what influence music might have—the self-taught genius played his invariable waltz, and, of course, was deemed worthy of the most flattering applause. Pricked on by rivalry, Count H., our incomparable dilettante (see Chapter I.), gave a little song of his own composition, cribbed wholesale from Offenbach. Its playful refrain to the words: '*Quel œuf? quel bœuf?*' set almost all the ladies' heads swinging to right and to left; one went so far as to hum the tune lightly, and the irrepressible, inevitable word, '*Charmant! charmant!*' was fluttering on every one's lips. Irina exchanged a glance with Litvinov, and again the same secret, ironical expression quivered about her lips. . . . But a little later it was still more strongly marked, there was even a shade of malice in it, when Prince Kokó, that representative and champion of the interests of the nobility, thought fit to propound his views to the spiritualist, and, of course, gave utterance before long to his famous phrase about the shock to the principle of property, accompanied naturally by an attack on democrats. The spiritualist's American blood was stirred; he began to argue. The prince, as his habit was, at once fell to shouting at the top of his voice; instead of any kind of argument he repeated incessantly: '*C'est absurde! cela n'a pas le sens commun!*' The millionaire Finikov began saying insulting things, without much heed to whom they referred; the Talmudist's piping notes and even the Countess S.'s jarring voice could be heard. . . . In fact, almost the same incongruous uproar arose as at Gubaryov's; the only difference was that here there was no beer nor tobacco-smoke, and every one was better dressed. Ratmirov tried to restore tranquillity (the generals manifested their displeasure, Boris's exclamation could be heard, '*Encore cette satanée politique!*'), but his efforts were not successful, and at that point, a high official of the stealthily inquisitorial type, who was present, and undertook to present *le résumé en peu de mots*, sustained a defeat: in fact he so hummed and hawed, so repeated himself, and was so obviously incapable of listening to or taking in the answers he received, and so unmistakably failed to perceive himself what precisely constituted *la question* that no other result could possibly have been anticipated. And then too Irina was slily provoking the disputants and setting them against one another, constantly exchanging glances and slight signs with Litvinov as she did so. . . . But he was sitting like one spell-bound, he was hearing nothing, and waiting for nothing but for those splendid eyes to sparkle again, that pale, tender, mischievous, exquisite face to flash upon him again. . . . It ended by the ladies growing restive, and requesting that the dispute should cease. . . . Ratmirov entreated the dilettante to sing his song again, and the self-taught genius once more played his waltz. . . .

Litvinov stayed till after midnight, and went away later than all the rest. The conversation had in the course of the evening touched upon a number of subjects, studiously avoiding anything of the faintest interest; the generals, after finishing their solemn game, solemnly joined in it: the influence of these statesmen was at once apparent. The conversation turned upon notorieties of the Parisian demi-monde, with whose names and talents every one seemed intimately acquainted, on Sardou's latest play, on a novel of About's, on Patti in the *Traviata*. Some one proposed a game of 'secretary,' *au secrétaire;* but it was not a success. The answers given were pointless, and often not free from grammatical mistakes; the stout general related that he had once in answer to the question: *Qu'est-ce que l'amour?* replied, *Une colique remontée au cœur,* and promptly went off into his wooden guffaw; the ancient ruin with a mighty effort struck him with her fan on the arm; a flake of plaster was shaken off her forehead by this rash action. The old crone was beginning a reference to the Slavonic principalities and the necessity of orthodox propaganda on the Danube, but, meeting with no response, she subsided with a hiss. In reality they talked more about Home than anything else; even the 'Queen of the Wasps' described how hands had once crept about her, and how she had seen them, and put her own ring on one of them. It was certainly a triumph for Irina: even if Litvinov had paid more attention to what was being said around him, he still could not have gleaned one single sincere saying, one single clever thought, one single new fact from all their disconnected and lifeless babble. Even in their cries and exclamations, there was no note of real feeling, in their slander no real heat. Only at rare intervals under the mask of assumed patriotic indignation, or of assumed contempt and indifference, the dread of possible losses could be heard in a plaintive whimper, and a few names, which will not be forgotten by posterity, were pronounced with gnashing of teeth . . . And not a drop of living water under all this noise and wrangle! What stale, what unprofitable nonsense, what wretched trivialities were absorbing all these heads and hearts, and not for that one evening, not in society only, but at home too, every hour and every day, in all the depth and breadth of their existence! And what ignorance, when all is said! What lack of understanding of all on which human life is built, all by which life is made beautiful!

On parting from Litvinov, Irina again pressed his hand and whispered significantly, 'Well? Are you pleased? Have you seen enough? Do you like it?' He made her no reply, but merely bowed low in silence.

Left alone with her husband, Irina was just going to her bedroom. . . . He stopped her.

'*Je vous ai beaucoup admirée ce soir, madame,*' he observed, smoking a cigarette, and leaning against the mantelpiece, '*vous vous êtes parfaitement moquée de nous tous.*'

'*Pas plus cette fois-ci que les autres,*' she answered indifferently.

'How do you mean me to understand you?' asked Ratmirov.

'As you like.'

'Hm. *C'est clair.*' Ratmirov warily, like a cat, knocked off the ash of the cigarette with the tip of the long nail of his little finger. 'Oh, by the way! This new friend of yours—what the dickens is his name?—Mr. Litvinov—doubtless enjoys the reputation of a very clever man.'

At the name of Litvinov, Irina turned quickly round.

'What do you mean to say?'

The general smiled.

'He keeps very quiet . . . one can see he's afraid of compromising himself.'

Irina too smiled; it was a very different smile from her husband's.

'Better keep quiet than talk . . . as some people talk.'

'*Attrapé!*' answered Ratmirov with feigned submissiveness. 'Joking apart, he has a very interesting face. Such a . . . concentrated expression . . . and his whole bearing. . . . Yes. . . .' The general straightened his cravat, and bending his head stared at his own moustache. 'He's a republican, I imagine, of the same sort as your other friend, Mr. Potugin; that's another of your clever fellows who are dumb.'

Irina's brows were slowly raised above her wide open clear eyes, while her lips were tightly pressed together and faintly curved.

'What's your object in saying that, Valerian

Vladimiritch,' she remarked, as though sympathetically. 'You are wasting your arrows on the empty air. . . . We are not in Russia, and there is no one to hear you.'

Ratmirov was stung.

'That's not merely my opinion, Irina Pavlovna,' he began in a voice suddenly guttural; 'other people too notice that that gentleman has the air of a conspirator.'

'Really? who are these other people?'

'Well, Boris for instance——'

'What? was it necessary for him too to express his opinion?'

Irina shrugged her shoulders as though shrinking from the cold, and slowly passed the tips of her fingers over them.

'Him . . . yes, him. Allow me to remark, Irina Pavlovna, that you seem angry; and you know if one is angry——'

'Am I angry? Oh, what for?'

'I don't know; possibly you have been disagreeably affected by the observation I permitted myself to make in reference to——'

Ratmirov stammered.

'In reference to?' Irina repeated interrogatively. 'Ah, if you please, no irony, and make haste. I'm tired and sleepy.'

She took a candle from the table. 'In reference to——?'

'Well, in reference to this same Mr. Litvinov; since there's no doubt now that you take a great interest in him.'

Irina lifted the hand in which she was holding the candlestick, till the flame was brought on a level with her husband's face, and attentively, almost with curiosity, looking him straight in the face, she suddenly burst into laughter.

'What is it?' asked Ratmirov scowling.

Irina went on laughing.

'Well, what is it?' he repeated, and he stamped his foot.

He felt insulted, wounded, and at the same time against his will he was impressed by the beauty of this woman, standing so lightly and boldly before him . . . she was tormenting him. He saw everything, all her charms—even the pink reflection of the delicate nails on her slender finger-tips, as they tightly clasped the dark bronze of the heavy candlestick — even that did not escape him . . . while the insult cut deeper and deeper into his heart. And still Irina laughed.

'What? you? you jealous?' she brought out at last, and turning her back on her husband she went out of the room. 'He's jealous!' he heard outside the door, and again came the sound of her laugh.

Ratmirov looked moodily after his wife; he

could not even then help noticing the bewitching grace of her figure, her movements, and with a violent blow, crushing the cigarette on the marble slab of the mantelpiece, he flung it to a distance. His cheeks had suddenly turned white, a spasm passed over the lower half of his face, and with a dull animal stare his eyes strayed about the floor, as though in search of something. . . . Every semblance of refinement had vanished from his face. Such an expression it must have worn when he was flogging the White Russian peasants.

Litvinov had gone home to his rooms, and sitting down to the table he had buried his head in both hands, and remained a long while without stirring. He got up at last, opened a box, and taking out a pocket-book, he drew out of an inner pocket a photograph of Tatyana. Her face gazed out mournfully at him, looking ugly and old, as photographs usually do. Litvinov's betrothed was a girl of Great Russian blood, a blonde, rather plump, and with the features of her face rather heavy, but with a wonderful expression of kindness and goodness in her intelligent, clear brown eyes, with a serene, white brow, on which it seemed as though a sunbeam always rested. For a long time Litvinov did not take his eyes from the photograph, then he pushed it gently away and again clutched his head in both hands. 'All is at an end!' he whispered at last, 'Irina! Irina!'

Only now, only at that instant, he realised that he was irrevocably, senselessly, in love with her, that he had loved her since the very day of that first meeting with her at the Old Castle, that he had never ceased to love her. And yet how astounded, how incredulous, how scornful, he would have been, had he been told so a few hours back!

'But Tanya, Tanya, my God! Tanya! Tanya!' he repeated in contrition; while Irina's shape fairly rose before his eyes in her black almost funereal garb, with the radiant calm of victory on her marble white face.

XVI

LITVINOV did not sleep all night, and did not undress. He was very miserable. As an honest and straightforward man, he realised the force of obligations, the sacredness of duty, and would have been ashamed of any double dealing with himself, his weakness, his fault. At first he was overcome by apathy; it was long before he could throw off the gloomy burden of a single half-conscious, obscure sensation; then terror took possession of him at the thought that the future, his almost conquered future, had slipped back into the darkness, that his home, the solidly-built home he had only just raised, was suddenly tottering about him. . . .

He began reproaching himself without mercy, but at once checked his own vehemence. 'What feebleness!' he thought. 'It's no time for self-reproach and cowardice; now I must act. Tanya is my betrothed, she has faith in my love, my honour, we are bound together for life, and cannot, must not, be put asunder.' He vividly pictured to himself all Tanya's qualities, mentally he picked them out and reckoned them up; he was trying to call up feeling and tenderness in himself. 'One thing's left for me,' he thought again, 'to run away, to run away directly, without waiting for her arrival, to hasten to meet her; whether I suffer, whether I am wretched with Tanya—that's not likely—but in any case to think of that, to take that into consideration is useless; I must do my duty, if I die for it! But you have no right to deceive her,' whispered another voice within him. 'You have no right to hide from her the change in your feelings; it may be that when she knows you love another woman, she will not be willing to become your wife? Rubbish! rubbish!' he answered, 'that's all sophistry, shameful double-dealing, deceitful conscientiousness; I have no right not to keep my word, that's the thing. Well, so be it. . . . Then I must go away from here, without seeing the other. . . .'

But at that point Litvinov's heart throbbed with anguish, he turned cold, physically cold, a momentary shiver passed over him, his teeth chattered weakly. He stretched and yawned, as though he were in a fever. Without dwelling longer on his last thought, choking back that thought, turning away from it, he set himself to marvelling and wondering in perplexity how he could again . . . again love that corrupt worldly creature, all of whose surroundings were so hateful, so repulsive to him. He tried to put to himself the question: 'What nonsense, do you really love her?' and could only wring his hands in despair. He was still marvelling and wondering, and suddenly there rose up before his eyes, as though from a soft fragrant mist, a seductive shape, shining eyelashes were lifted, and softly and irresistibly the marvellous eyes pierced him to the heart and a voice was singing with sweetness in his ears, and resplendent shoulders, the shoulders of a young queen, were breathing with voluptuous freshness and warmth. . . .

Towards morning a determination was at last fully formed in Litvinov's mind. He decided to set off that day to meet Tatyana, and seeing Irina for the last time, to tell her, since there was nothing else for it, the whole truth, and to part from her for ever.

He set in order and packed his things, waited till twelve o'clock, and started to go to her. But at the sight of her half-curtained windows Litvinov's heart fairly failed him . . . he could not summon up courage to enter the hotel. He walked once or twice up and down Lichtenthaler Allee. 'A very good day to Mr. Litvinov!'

he suddenly heard an ironical voice call from the top of a swiftly-moving 'dogcart.' Litvinov raised his eyes and saw General Ratmirov sitting beside Prince M., a well-known sportsman and fancier of English carriages and horses. The prince was driving, the general was leaning over on one side, grinning, while he lifted his hat high above his head. Litvinov bowed to him, and at the same instant, as though he were obeying a secret command, he set off at a run towards Irina's.

She was at home. He sent up his name; he was at once received. When he went in, she was standing in the middle of the room. She was wearing a morning blouse with wide open sleeves; her face, pale as the day before, but not fresh as it had been then, expressed weariness; the languid smile with which she welcomed her visitor emphasised that expression even more clearly. She held out her hand to him in a friendly way, but absent-mindedly.

'Thanks for coming,' she began in a plaintive voice, and she sank into a low chair. 'I am not very well this morning; I spent a bad night. Well, what have you to say about last night? Wasn't I right?'

Litvinov sat down.

'I have come to you, Irina Pavlovna,' he began.

She instantly sat up and turned round; her eyes simply fastened upon Litvinov.

'What is it,' she cried. 'You're pale as death, you're ill. What's the matter with you?'

Litvinov was confused.

'With me, Irina Pavlovna?'

'Have you had bad news? Some misfortune has happened, tell me, tell me——'

Litvinov in his turn looked at Irina.

'I have had no bad news,' he brought out not without effort, 'but a misfortune has certainly happened, a great misfortune . . . and it has brought me to you.'

'A misfortune? What is it?'

'Why . . . that——'

Litvinov tried to go on . . . and could not. He only pinched his hands together so that his fingers cracked. Irina was bending forward and seemed turned to stone.

'Oh! I love you!' broke at last with a low groan from Litvinov's breast, and he turned away, as though he would hide his face.

'What, Grigory Mihalitch, you' . . . Irina too could not finish her sentence, and leaning back in her chair, she put both her hands to her eyes. 'You . . . love me.'

'Yes . . . yes . . . yes,' he repeated with bitterness, turning his head further and further away.

Everything was silent in the room; a butterfly that had flown in was fluttering its wings and struggling between the curtain and the window.

The first to speak was Litvinov.

'That, Irina Pavlovna,' he began, 'that is the misfortune, which . . . has befallen me, which I ought to have foreseen and avoided, if I had not now just as in the Moscow days been carried off my feet at once. It seems fate is pleased to force me once again through you to suffer tortures, which one would have thought should not be repeated again. . . . It was not without cause I struggled. . . . I tried to struggle; but of course there's no escaping one's fate. And I tell you all this to put an end at once to this . . . this tragic farce,' he added with a fresh outburst of shame and bitterness.

Litvinov was silent again; the butterfly was struggling and fluttering as before. Irina did not take her hands from her face.

'And you are not mistaken?' her whisper sounded from under those white, bloodless-looking hands.

'I am not mistaken,' answered Litvinov in a colourless voice. 'I love you, as I have never loved any one but you. I am not going to reproach you; that would be too foolish; I'm not going to tell you that perhaps nothing of all this would have happened if you yourself had behaved differently with me. . . . Of course, I alone am to blame, my self-confidence has been my ruin; I am deservedly punished, and you could not have anticipated it. Of course you did not consider that it would have been far less dangerous for me if you had not been so keenly alive to your wrong . . . your supposed wrong to me; and had not wished to make up for it . . . but what's done can't be undone. I only wanted to make clear my position to you; it's hard enough as it is. . . . But at least there will be, as you say, no misunderstanding, while the openness of my confession will soften, I hope, the feeling of offence which you cannot but feel.'

Litvinov spoke without raising his eyes, but even if he had glanced at Irina, he could not have seen what was passing in her face, as she still as before kept her hands over her eyes. But what was passing over her face meanwhile would probably have astounded him; both alarm and delight were apparent on it, and a kind of blissful helplessness and agitation; her eyes hardly glimmered under their overhanging lids, and her slow, broken breathing was chill upon her lips, that were parted as though with thirst. . . .

Litvinov was silent, waiting for a response, some sound. . . . Nothing!

'There is one thing left for me,' he began again, 'to go away; I have come to say good-bye to you.'

Irina slowly dropped her hands on to her knees.

'But I remember, Grigory Mihalitch,' she began; 'that . . . that person of whom you spoke to me, she was to have come here? You are expecting her?'

'Yes; but I shall write to her . . . she will stop somewhere on the way . . . at Heidelberg, for instance.'

'Ah! Heidelberg. . . . Yes. . . . It's nice there. . . . But all this must upset your plans. Are you perfectly certain, Grigory Mihalitch, that you are not exaggerating, *et que ce n'est pas une fausse alarme*?'

Irina spoke softly, almost coldly, with short pauses, looking away towards the window. Litvinov made no answer to her last question.

'Only, why did you talk of offence?' she went on. 'I am not offended . . . oh, no! and if one or other of us is to blame, in any case it's not you; not you alone. . . . Remember our last conversations, and you will be convinced that it's not you who are to blame.'

'I have never doubted your magnanimity,

Litvinov muttered between his teeth, 'but I should like to know, do you approve of my intention?'

'To go away?'

'Yes.'

Irina continued to look away.

'At the first moment, your intention struck me as premature. . . . but now I have thought over what you have said . . . and if you are really not mistaken, then I suppose that you ought to go away. It will be better so . . better for us both.'

Irina's voice had grown lower and lower, and her words too came more and more slowly.

'General Ratmirov, certainly, might notice,' Litvinov was beginning. . . .

Irina's eyes dropped again, and something strange quivered about her lips, quivered and died away.

'No; you did not understand me,' she interrupted him. 'I was not thinking of my husband. Why should I? And there is nothing to notice. But I repeat, separation is necessary for us both.'

Litvinov picked up his hat, which had fallen on the ground.

'Everything is over,' he thought, 'I must go. And so it only remains for me to say good-bye to you, Irina Pavlovna,' he said aloud, and suddenly felt a pang, as though he were preparing to pronounce his own sentence on himself. 'It only remains for me to hope that you will not remember evil against me, and . . . and that if we ever——'

Irina again cut him short.

'Wait a little, Grigory Mihalitch, don't say good-bye to me yet. That would be too hurried.'

Something wavered in Litvinov, but the burning pain broke out again and with redoubled violence in his heart.

'But I can't stay,' he cried. 'What for? Why prolong this torture?'

'Don't say good-bye to me yet,' repeated Irina. 'I must see you once more. . . . Another such dumb parting as in Moscow again—no, I don't want that. You can go now, but you must promise me, give me your word of honour that you won't go away without seeing me once more.'

'You wish that?'

'I insist on it. If you go away without saying good-bye to me, I shall never forgive it, do you hear, never! Strange!' she added as though to herself, 'I cannot persuade myself that I am in Baden. . . . I keep feeling that I am in Moscow. . . . Go now.'

Litvinov got up.

'Irina Pavlovna,' he said, 'give me your hand.'

Irina shook her head.

'I told you that I don't want to say goodbye to you. . . .

'I don't ask it for that.'

Irina was about to stretch out her hand, but she glanced at Litvinov for the first time since his avowal, and drew it back.

'No, no,' she whispered, 'I will not give you my hand. No . . . no. Go now.'

Litvinov bowed and went away. He could not tell why Irina had refused him that last friendly handshake. . . He could not know what she feared.

He went away, and Irina again sank into the armchair and again covered her face.

XVII

LITVINOV did not return home; he went up to the hills, and getting into a thick copse, he flung himself face downwards on the earth, and lay there about an hour. He did not suffer tortures, did not weep; he sank into a kind of heavy, oppressive stupor. Never had he felt anything like it; it was an insufferably aching and gnawing sensation of emptiness, emptiness in himself, his surroundings, everywhere. . . . He thought neither of Irina nor of Tatyana. He felt one thing only: a blow had fallen and life was sundered like a cord, and all of him was being drawn along in the clutches of something chill and unfamiliar. Sometimes it seemed to him that a whirlwind had swooped down upon him, and he had the sensation of its swift whirling round and the irregular beating of its dark wings. But his resolution did not waver. To remain in Baden . . .that could not even be considered. In thought he had already gone, he was already sitting in the rattling, snorting train, hurrying, hurrying into the dumb, dead distance. He got up at last, and leaning his head against a tree, stayed motionless; only with one hand, he all unconsciously snatched and swung in rhythm the topmost frond of a fern. The sound of approaching footsteps drew him out of his stupor: two charcoal-burners were making their way down the steep path with large sacks on their shoulders. 'It's time!' whispered Litvinov, and he followed the charcoal-burners to the town, turned into the railway station, and sent off a telegram to Tatyana's aunt, Kapitolina Markovna. In this telegram he informed her of his immediate departure, and appointed as a meeting-place, Schrader's hotel in Heidelberg.

'Make an end, make an end at once,' he thought; 'it's useless putting it off till tomorrow.' Then he went to the gambling saloon, stared with dull curiosity at the faces of two or three gamblers, got a back view of Bindasov's ugly head in the distance, noticed the irreproachable countenance of Pishtchalkin, and after waiting a little under the colonnade, he set off deliberately to Irina's. He was not going to her through the force of sudden, involuntary temptation; when he made up his mind to go away, he also made up his mind to keep his word and see her once more.

He went into the hotel unobserved by the porter, ascended the staircase, not meeting any one, and without knocking at the door, he mechanically pushed it open and went into the room.

In the room, in the same armchair, in the same dress, in precisely the same attitude as three hours before, was sitting Irina. . . . It was obvious that she had not moved from the place, had not stirred all that time. She slowly raised her head, and seeing Litvinov, she trembled all over and clutched the arm of the chair. 'You frightened me,' she whispered.

Litvinov looked at her with speechless bewilderment. The expression of her face, her lustreless eyes, astounded him.

Irina gave a forced smile and smoothed her ruffled hair. 'Never mind. . . . I really don't know. . . . I think I must have fallen asleep here.'

'I beg your pardon, Irina Pavlovna,' began Litvinov. 'I came in unannounced. . . . I wanted to do what you thought fit to require of me. So as I am going away to-day——'

'To-day? But I thought you told me that you meant first to write a letter——'

'I have sent a telegram.'

'Ah! you found it necessary to make haste. And when are you going? What time, I mean?'

'At seven o'clock this evening.'

'Ah! at seven o'clock! And you have come to say good-bye?'

'Yes, Irina Pavlovna, to say good-bye.'

Irina was silent for a little.

'I ought to thank you, Grigory Mihalitch, it was probably not easy for you to come here.'

'No, Irina Pavlovna, it was anything but easy.'

'Life is not generally easy, Grigory Mihalitch; what do you think about it?'

'It depends, Irina Pavlovna.'

Irina was silent again for a little; she seemed sunk in thought.

'You have proved your affection for me by coming,' she said at last, 'I thank you. And I fully approve of your decision to put an end to everything as soon as possible . . . because any delay . . . because . . . because I, even I whom you have reproached as a flirt, called an actress . . . that, I think, was what you called me? . . .'

Irina got up swiftly, and, sitting down in another chair, stooped down and pressed her face and arms on the edge of the table.

'Because I love you . . .' she whispered between her clasped fingers.

Litvinov staggered, as though some one had dealt him a blow in the chest. Irina turned her head dejectedly away from him, as though she in her turn wanted to hide her face from him, and laid it down on the table.

'Yes, I love you ... I love you ... and you know it.'

'I? I know it?' Litvinov said at last; 'I?'

'Well, now you see,' Irina went on, 'that you certainly must go, that delay's impossible ... both for you, and for me delay's impossible. It's dangerous, it's terrible ... good-bye!' she added, rising impulsively from her chair, 'good-bye!'

She took a few steps in the direction of the door of her boudoir, and putting her hand behind her back, made a hurried movement in the air, as though she would find and press the hand of Litvinov; but he stood like a block of wood, at a distance.... Once more she said, 'Good-bye, forget me,' and without looking round she rushed away.

Litvinov remained alone, and yet still could not come to himself. He recovered himself at last, went quickly to the boudoir door, uttered Irina's name once, twice, three times ... He had already his hand on the lock ... From the hotel stairs rose the sound of Ratmirov's sonorous voice.

Litvinov pulled down his hat over his eyes, and went out on to the staircase. The elegant general was standing before the Swiss porter's box and explaining to him in bad German that he wanted a hired carriage for the whole of the next day. On catching sight of Litvinov, he again lifted his hat unnaturally high, and again wished him 'a very good-day'; he was obviously jeering at him, but Litvinov had no thoughts for that. He hardly responded to Ratmirov's bow, and, making his way to his lodging, he stood still before his already packed and closed trunk. His head was turning round and his heart vibrating like a harp-string. What was to be done now? And could he have foreseen this?

Yes, he had foreseen it, however unlikely it seemed. It had stunned him like a clap of thunder, yet he had foreseen it, though he had not courage even to acknowledge it. Besides he knew nothing now for certain. Everything was confusion and turmoil within him; he had lost the thread of his own thoughts. He remembered Moscow, he remembered how then too 'it' had come upon him like a sudden tempest. He was breathless; rapture, but a rapture comfortless and hopeless, oppressed and tore his heart. For nothing in the world would he have consented that the words uttered by Irina should not have actually been uttered by her.... But then? those words could not for all that change the resolution he had taken. As before, it did not waver; it stood firm like an anchor. Litvinov had lost the thread of his own thoughts . . . yes; but his will still remained to him, and he disposed of himself as of another man dependent on him. He rang for the waiter, asked him for the bill, bespoke a place in the evening omnibus; designedly he cut himself off all paths of retreat. 'If I die for it after!' he declared, as he had in the previous sleepless night; that phrase seemed especially to his taste. 'Then even if I die for it!' he repeated, walking slowly up and down the room, and only at rare intervals, unconsciously, he shut his eyes and held his breath, while those words, those words of Irina's forced their way into his soul, and set it aflame. 'It seems you won't love twice,' he thought; 'another life came to you, you let it come into yours—never to be rid of that poison to the end, you will never break those bonds! Yes; but what does that prove? Happiness? . . . Is it possible? You love her, granted . . . and she . . . she loves you . . .'

But at this point again he had to pull himself up. As a traveller on a dark night, seeing before him a light, and afraid of losing the path, never for an instant takes his eyes off it, so Litvinov continually bent all the force of his attention on a single point, a single aim. To reach his betrothed, and not precisely even his betrothed (he was trying not to think of her) but to reach a room in the Heidelberg hotel, that was what stood immovably before him, a guiding light. What would be later, he did not know, nor did he want to know . . . One thing was beyond doubt, he would not come back. 'If I die first!' he repeated for the tenth time, and he glanced at his watch.

A quarter-past six! How long still to wait! He paced once more up and down. The sun was nearly setting, the sky was crimson above the trees, and the pink flush of twilight lay on the narrow windows of his darkening room. Suddenly Litvinov fancied the door had been opened quickly and softly behind him and as quickly closed again . . . He turned round; at the door, muffled in a dark cloak, was standing a woman . . .

'Irina,' he cried, and clapped his hands together in amazement . . . She raised her head and fell upon his breast.

Two hours later he was sitting in his room on the sofa. His box stood in the corner, open and empty, and on the table in the midst of things flung about in disorder, lay a letter from Tatyana, just received by him. She wrote to him that she had decided to hasten her departure from Dresden, since her aunt's health was completely restored, and that if nothing happened to delay them, they would both be in Baden the following day at twelve o'clock, and hoped that he would come to meet them at the station. Apartments had already been taken for them by Litvinov in the same hotel in which he was staying.

The same evening he sent a note to Irina, and the following morning he received a reply from her. 'Sooner or later,' she wrote, 'it must have been. I tell you again what I said yesterday: my life is in your hands, do with me what you will. I do not want to hamper your freedom, but let me say, that if necessary, I will throw up everything, and follow you to the ends of the earth. We shall see each other to-morrow, of course.—Your Irina.'

The last two words were written in a large, bold, resolute hand.

XVIII

AMONG the persons assembled on the 18th of August at twelve o'clock on the platform at the railway station was Litvinov. Not long before, he had seen Irina: she was sitting in an open carriage with her husband and another gentleman, somewhat elderly. She caught sight of Litvinov, and he perceived that some obscure emotion flitted over her eyes; but at once she hid herself from him with her parasol.

A strange transformation had taken place in him since the previous day — in his whole appearance, his movements, the expression of his face; and indeed he felt himself a different man. His self-confidence had vanished, and his peace of mind had vanished too, and his respect for himself; of his former spiritual condition nothing was left. Recent ineffaceable impressions obscured all the rest from him Some sensation unknown before had come, strong, sweet—and evil; the mysterious guest had made its way to the innermost shrine and taken possession and lain down in it, in silence, but in all its magnitude, like the owner in a new house. Litvinov was no longer ashamed, he was afraid; at the same time a desperate hardihood had sprung up in him; the captured, the vanquished know well this mixture of opposing feelings; the thief too knows something of it after his first robbery. Litvinov had been vanquished, vanquished suddenly ... and what had become of his honesty?

The train was a few minutes late. Litvinov's suspense passed into agonising torture; he could not stop still in one place, and, pale all over, moved about jostling in the crowd. 'My God,' he thought, 'if I only had another twenty-four hours' ... The first look at Tanya, the first look of Tanya ... that was what filled him with terror ... that was what he had to live through directly ... And afterwards? Afterwards ... come, what may come! . . He now made no more resolutions, he could not answer for himself now. His phrase of yesterday flashed painfully through his head ... And this was how he was meeting Tanya. ...

A prolonged whistle sounded at last, a heavy momentarily increasing rumble was heard, and, slowly rolling round a bend in the line, the train came into sight. The crowd hurried to meet it, and Litvinov followed it, dragging his feet like a condemned man. Faces, ladies' hats began to appear out of the carriages, at one window a white handkerchief gleamed. . . . Kapitolina Markovna was waving to him. . . . It was over; she had caught sight of Litvinov and he recognised her. The train stood still; Litvinov rushed to the carriage door, and opened it; Tatyana was standing near her aunt, smiling brightly and holding out her hand.

He helped them both to get out, uttered a few words of welcome, unfinished and confused, and at once bustled about, began taking their tickets, their travelling bags, and rugs, ran to find a porter, called a fly; other people were bustling around them. He was glad of their presence, their fuss, and loud talk. Tatyana moved a little aside, and, still smiling, waited calmly for his hurried arrangements to be concluded. Kapitolina Markovna, on the other hand, could not keep still; she could not believe that she was at last at Baden.

She suddenly cried, 'But the parasols? Tanya, where are our parasols?' all unconscious that she was holding them fast under her arm; then she began taking a loud and prolonged farewell of another lady with whom she had made friends on the journey from Heidelberg to Baden. This lady was no other than our old friend Madame Suhantchikov. She had gone away to Heidelberg to do obeisance to Gubaryov, and was returning with 'instructions.' Kapitolina Markovna wore a rather peculiar striped mantle and a round travelling hat of a mushroom-shape, from under which her short white hair fell in disorder; short and thin, she was flushed with travelling and kept talking Russian in a shrill and penetrating voice.... She was an object of attention at once.

Litvinov at last put her and Tatyana into a fly, and placed himself opposite them. The horses started. Then followed questionings, renewed handshaking, interchanging of smiles and welcomes... Litvinov breathed freely; the first moment had passed off satisfactorily. Nothing in him, apparently, had struck or bewildered Tanya; she was smiling just as brightly and confidently, she was blushing as charmingly, and laughing as goodnaturedly. He brought himself at last to take a look at her; not a stealthy cursory glance, but a direct steady look at her, hitherto his own eyes had refused to obey him. His heart throbbed with involuntary emotion: the serene expression of that honest, candid face gave him a pang of bitter reproach. 'So you are here, poor girl,' he thought, 'you whom I have so longed for, so urged to come, with whom I had hoped to spend my life to the end, you have come, you believed in me . . .

while I ... while I.' ... Litvinov's head sank; but Kapitolina Markovna gave him no time for musing; she was pelting him with questions.

'What is that building with columns? Where is it the gambling's done? Who is that coming along? Tanya, Tanya, look, what crinolines! And who can that be? I suppose they are mostly French creatures from Paris here? Mercy, what a hat! Can you get everything here just as in Paris? But, I expect, everything's awfully dear, eh? Ah, I've made the acquaintance of such a splendid, intellectual woman! You know her, Grigory Mihalitch; she told me she had met you at some Russian's, who's a wonderfully intellectual person too. She promised to come and see us. How she does abuse all these aristocrats—it's simply superb! What is that gentleman with grey moustaches? The Prussian king? Tanya, Tanya, look, that's the Prussian king. No? not the Prussian king, the Dutch ambassador, did you say? I can't hear, the wheels rattle so. Ah, what exquisite trees!'

'Yes, exquisite, aunt,' Tanya assented, 'and how green everything is here, how bright and gay! Isn't it, Grigory Mihalitch?'

'Oh, very bright and gay' ... he answered through his teeth.

The carriage stopped at last before the hotel.

Litvinov conducted the two travellers to the room taken for them, promised to come back within an hour, and went to his own room. Directly he entered it, he fell again under the spell which had been lulled for a while. Here, in that room, since the day before, Irina reigned supreme; everything was eloquent of her, the very air seemed to have kept secret traces of her visit. . . . Again Litvinov felt himself her slave. He drew out her handkerchief, hidden in his bosom, pressed it to his lips, and burning memories flowed in subtle poison through his veins. He realised that there was no turning back, no choosing now; the sorrowful emotion aroused in him by Tatyana melted away like snow in the fire, and remorse died down . . . died down so completely that his uneasiness even was soothed, and the possibility—present to his intellect—of hypocrisy no longer revolted him. . . . Love, Irina's love, that was now his truth, his bond, his conscience. . . . The sensible Litvinov did not even ponder how to get out of a position, the horror and hideousness of which he bore lightly, as if it did not concern him.

The hour had not yet passed when a waiter came to Litvinov from the newly arrived ladies; they begged him to come to them in the public drawing-room. He followed the messenger, and found them already dressed and in their hats. They both expressed a desire to go out at once to see Baden, as the weather was so fine. Kapitolina Markovna especially seemed burning with impatience; she was quite cast down when she heard that the hour of the fashionable promenade before the Konversation Hall had not yet arrived. Litvinov gave her his arm, and the ceremony of sight-seeing began. Tatyana walked beside her aunt, looking about her with quiet interest; Kapitolina Markovna pursued her inquiries. The sight of the roulette, the dignified croupiers, whom—had she met them in any other place—she would certainly have taken for ministers, the quickly moving scoops, the heaps of gold and silver on the green cloth, the old women gambling, and the painted *cocottes* reduced Kapitolina Markovna to a sort of speechless stupor; she altogether forgot that she ought to feel moral indignation, and could only gaze and gaze, giving a start of surprise at every new sight. . . . The whiz of the ivory ball into the bottom of the roulette thrilled her to the marrow of her bones, and it was only when she was again in the open air that, drawing a long breath, she recovered energy enough to denounce games of chance as an immoral invention of aristocracy. A fixed, unpleasant smile had made its appearance on Litvinov's lips; he had spoken abruptly and lazily, as though he were annoyed or bored. . . . But now he turned round towards Tatyana, and was thrown into secret confusion; she was looking attentively at him, with an expression as though she were asking herself what sort of an impression was being made on her. He made haste to nod his head to her, she responded with the same gesture, and again looked at him questioningly, with a sort of strained effort, as though he were standing much further off than he really was. Litvinov led his ladies away from the Konversation Hall, and passing the 'Russian tree,' under which two Russian ladies were already sitting, he went towards Lichtenthaler Allee. He had hardly entered the avenue when he saw Irina in the distance.

She was walking towards him with her husband and Potugin. Litvinov turned white as a sheet; he did not slacken his pace, however, and when he was on a level with her, he made a bow without speaking. She too bowed to him, politely, but coldly, and taking in Tatyana in a rapid glance, she glided by. . . . Ratmirov lifted his hat high, Potugin muttered something.

'Who is that lady?' Tatyana asked suddenly. Till that instant she had hardly opened her lips.

'That lady?' repeated Litvinov, 'that lady? That is a Madame Ratmirov.'

'Is she Russian?'

'Yes.'

'Did you make her acquaintance here?'

'No; I have known her a long while.'

'How beautiful she is!'

'Did you notice her dress?' put in Kapitolina Markovna. 'Ten families might live for a whole year on the cost of her lace alone. Was that her husband with her?' she inquired turning to Litvinov.

'Yes.'

'He must be awfully rich, I suppose?'

'Really I don't know; I don't think so.'

'What is his rank?'

'He's a general.'

'What eyes she has!' said Tatyana, 'and what a strange expression in them: pensive and penetrating at the same time. . . . I have never seen such eyes.'

Litvinov made no answer; he fancied that he felt again Tatyana's questioning glance bent on his face, but he was wrong, she was looking at her own feet, at the sand of the path.

'Mercy on us! Who is that fright?' cried Kapitolina Markovna suddenly, pointing to a low jaunting-car in which a red-haired pug-nosed woman lay lolling impudently, in an extraordinarily gorgeous costume and lilac stockings.

'That fright! why, that's the celebrated Ma'mselle Cora.'

'Who?'

'Ma'mselle Cora . . . a Parisian . . . notoriety.'

'What? That pug? Why, but she's hideous!'

'It seems that's no hindrance.'

Kapitolina Markovna could only lift her hands in astonishment.

'Well, this Baden of yours!' she brought out at last. 'Can one sit down on a seat here? I'm rather tired.'

'Of course you can, Kapitolina Markovna. . . . That's what the seats are put here for.'

'Well, really, there's no knowing! But there in Paris, I'm told, there are seats, too, along the boulevards; but it's not proper to sit on them.'

Litvinov made no reply to Kapitolina Markovna; only at that moment he realised that two paces away was the very spot where he had had that explanation with Irina, which had decided everything. Then he recalled that he had noticed a small rosy spot on her cheek to-day. . . .

Kapitolina Markovna sank down on to the seat, Tatyana sat down beside her. Litvinov remained on the path; between Tatyana and him—or was it only his fancy?—something seemed to have happened ... unconsciously and gradually.

'Ah, she's a wretch, a perfect wretch!' Kapitolina Markovna declared, shaking her head commiseratingly; 'why, with the price of *her* get-up, you could keep not ten, but a hundred families. Did you see under her hat, on her red hair, there were diamonds? Upon my word, diamonds in the day-time!'

'Her hair's not red,' remarked Litvinov; 'she dyes it red—that's the fashion now.'

Again Kapitolina Markovna could only lift her hands; she was positively dumbfounded.

'Well,' she said at last, 'where we were, in Dresden, things had not got to such a scandalous pitch yet. It's a little further from Paris, anyway, that's why. Don't you think that's it, Grigory Mihalitch, eh?'

'Don't I think so?' answered Litvinov. While he thought to himself, 'What on earth is she talking of?' 'I? Of course ... of course....'

But at this point the sound of slow footsteps was heard, and Potugin approached the seat.

'Good-morning, Grigory Mihalitch,' he began, smiling and nodding.

Litvinov grasped him by the hand at once.

'Good - morning, good - morning, Sozont Ivanitch. I fancy I passed you just now with ... just now in the avenue?'

'Yes, it was me.'

Potugin bowed respectfully to the ladies sitting on the seat.

'Let me introduce you, Sozont Ivanitch. Old friends and relatives of mine, who have only just arrived in Baden. Potugin, Sozont Ivanitch, a countryman of ours, also staying in Baden.'

Both ladies rose a little. Potugin renewed his bows.

'It's quite a levée here,' Kapitolina Markovna began in a delicate voice; the kind-hearted old lady was easily intimidated, but she tried before all to keep up her dignity. 'Every one regards it as an agreeable duty to stay here.'

'Baden is an agreeable place, certainly,' answered Potugin, with a sidelong look at Tatyana; 'a very agreeable place, Baden.'

'Yes; but it's really too aristocratic, so far as I can form an opinion. You see we have been staying all this time in Dresden ... a very interesting town; but here there's positively a levée.'

'She's pleased with the word,' thought Potugin. 'You are perfectly right in that observation,' he said aloud; 'but then the scenery here is exquisite, and the site of the place is something one cannot often find. Your fellow-traveller especially is sure to appreciate that. Are you not, madam?' he added, addressing himself this time directly to Tatyana.

Tatyana raised her large, clear eyes to Potugin. It seemed as though she were perplexed. What was wanted of her, and why had Litvinov introduced her, on the first day of her arrival, to this unknown man, who had, though, a kind and clever face, and was looking at her with cordial and friendly eyes.

'Yes,' she said at last, 'it's very nice here.'

'You ought to visit the old castle,' Potugin went on; 'I especially advise a drive to——'

'The Saxon Switzerland——' Kapitolina Markovna was beginning.

The blare of wind instruments floated up the avenue; it was the Prussian military band from Rastadt (in 1862 Rastadt was still an allied fortress), beginning its weekly concert in the pavilion. Kapitolina Markovna got up.

'The music!' she said; 'the music *à la Conversation*!... We must go there. It's four o'clock now... isn't it? Will the fashionable world be there now?'

'Yes,' answered Potugin: 'this is the most fashionable time, and the music is excellent.'

'Well, then, don't let us linger. Tanya, come along.'

'You allow me to accompany you?' asked Potugin, to Litvinov's considerable astonishment; it was not possible for it even to enter his head that Irina had sent Potugin.

Kapitolina Markovna simpered.

'With the greatest pleasure—M'sieu . . . M'sieu——'

'Potugin,' he murmured, and he offered her his arm.

Litvinov gave his to Tatyana, and both couples walked towards the Konversation Hall.

Potugin went on talking with Kapitolina Markovna. But Litvinov walked without uttering a word; yet twice, without any cause, he smiled, and faintly pressed Tatyana's arm against his. There was a falsehood in those demonstrations, to which she made no response, and Litvinov was conscious of the lie. They did not express a mutual confidence in the close union of two souls given up to one another; they were a temporary substitute—for words which he could not find. That unspoken something which was beginning between them grew and gained strength. Once more Tatyana looked attentively, almost intently, at him.

It was the same before the Konversation Hall at the little table round which they all four seated themselves, with this sole difference, that, in the noisy bustle of the crowd, the clash and roar of the music, Litvinov's silence seemed more comprehensible. Kapitolina Markovna became quite excited; Potugin hardly had time to answer her questions, to satisfy her curiosity. Luckily for him, there suddenly appeared in the mass of moving figures the lank person and everlastingly leaping eyes of Madame Suhantchikov. Kapitolina Markovna at once recognised her, invited her to their table, made her sit down, and a hurricane of words arose.

Potugin turned to Tatyana, and began a conversation with her in a soft, subdued voice, his face bent slightly down towards her with a very friendly expression; and she, to her own surprise, answered him easily and freely; she was glad to talk with this stranger, this outsider, while Litvinov sat immovable as before, with the same fixed and unpleasant smile on his lips.

Dinner-time came at last. The music ceased, the crowd thinned. Kapitolina Markovna parted from Madame Suhantchikov on the warmest terms. She had conceived an immense respect for her, though she did say afterwards to her niece, that 'this person is really too severe; but then she does know everything and everybody; and we must really get sewing-machines directly the wedding festivities are over.' Potugin took leave of them; Litvinov conducted his ladies home. As they were going into the hotel, he was handed a note; he moved aside and hurriedly tore open the envelope. On a tiny scrap of vellum paper were the following words, scribbled in pencil: 'Come to me this evening at seven, for one minute, I entreat you. —Irina.' Litvinov thrust the note into his pocket, and, turning round, put on his smile again . . . to whom? why? Tatyana was standing with her back to him. They dined at the common table of the hotel. Litvinov was sitting between Kapitolina Markovna and Tatyana, and he began talking, telling anecdotes and pouring out wine for himself and the ladies, with a strange, sudden joviality. He conducted himself in such a free and easy manner, that a French infantry officer from Strasbourg, sitting opposite, with a beard and moustaches *à la* Napoleon III., thought it admissible to join in the conversation, and even wound up by a toast *à la santé des belles Moscovites*! After dinner, Litvinov escorted the two ladies to their room, and after standing a little while at the window with a scowl on his face, he suddenly announced that he had to go out for a short time on business, but would be back without fail by the evening. Tatyana said nothing; she turned pale and dropped her eyes. Kapitolina Markovna was in the habit of taking a nap after dinner; Tatyana was well aware that Litvinov knew of this habit of her aunt's; she had expected him to take advantage of it, to remain with her, for he had not been alone with her, nor spoken frankly to her, since her arrival. And now he was going out! What was she to make of it? And, indeed, his whole behaviour all along. . . .

Litvinov withdrew hurriedly, not waiting for remonstrances; Kapitolina Markovna lay down on the sofa, and with one or two sighs and groans, fell into a serene sleep; while Tatyana moved away into a corner, and sat down in a low chair, folding her arms tightly across her bosom.

XIX

LITVINOV went quickly up the staircase of the *Hôtel de l'Europe*; a little girl of thirteen, with a sly little face of Kalmuck cast, who had apparently been on the look-out for him, stopped him, saying in Russian: 'Come this way, please; Irina Pavlovna will be here directly.' He looked at her in perplexity. She smiled, repeated: 'Come along, come along,' and led him to a small room, facing Irina's bedroom, and filled with travelling trunks and portmanteaus, then at once disappeared, closing the door very softly. Litvinov had not time to look about him, before the door was quickly opened, and before him in a pink ball-dress, with pearls in her hair and on her neck, stood Irina. She simply rushed at him, clutched him by both hands, and for a few instants was speechless; her eyes were shining, and her bosom heaving as though she had run up to a height.

'I could not receive . . . you there,' she began in a hurried whisper: 'we are just going to a dinner party, but I wanted above everything to see you. . . . That is your betrothed, I suppose, with whom I met you to-day?'

'Yes, that was my betrothed,' said Litvinov, with emphasis on the word 'was.'

'And so I wanted to see you for one minute, to tell you that you must consider yourself absolutely free, that everything that happened yesterday ought not to affect your plans. . . .'

'Irina!' cried Litvinov, 'why are you saying this?' He uttered these words in a loud voice. There was the note in them of unbounded passion. Irina involuntarily closed her eyes for a minute.

'Oh, my sweet one!' she went on in a whisper still more subdued, but with unrestrained emotion, 'you don't know how I love you, but yesterday I only paid my debt, I made up for the past. . . . Ah! I could not give you back my youth, as I would, but I have laid no obligations on you, I have exacted no promise of any sort of you, my sweet! Do what you will, you are free as air, you are bound in no way, understand that, understand that!'

'But I can't live without you, Irina,' Litvinov interrupted, in a whisper now; 'I am yours for ever and always, since yesterday. . . . I can only breathe at your feet. . . .'

He stooped down all in a tremble to kiss her hands. Irina gazed at his bent head.

'Then let me say,' she said, 'that I too am ready for anything, that I too will consider no one, and nothing. As you decide, so it shall be. I, too, am for ever yours . . . yours.'

Some one tapped warily at the door. Irina stooped, whispered once more, 'Yours . . . good-bye!' Litvinov felt her breath on his hair, the touch of her lips. When he stood up, she was no longer in the room, but her dress was rustling in the corridor, and from the distance came the voice of Ratmirov: '*Eh bien? Vous ne venez pas?*'

Litvinov sat down on a high chest, and hid his face. A feminine fragrance, fresh and delicate, clung about him. . . . Irina had held his hand in her hands. 'It's too much, too much,' was his thought. The little girl came into the room, and smiling again in response to his agitated glance, said:

'Kindly come, now——'

He got up, and went out of the hotel. It was no good even to think of returning home: he had to regain his balance first. His heart was beating heavily and unevenly; the earth seemed faintly reeling under his feet. Litvinov turned again along the Lichtenthaler Allee. He realised that the decisive moment had come, that to put it off longer, to dissemble, to turn away, had become impossible, that an explanation with Tatyana had become inevitable; he could imagine how she was sitting there, never stirring, waiting for him . . . he could foresee what he would say to her; but how was he to act, how was he to begin? He had turned his back on his upright, well-organised, orderly future; he knew that he was flinging himself headlong into a gulf . . . but that did not confound him. The thing was done, but how was he to face his judge? And if only his judge would come to meet him—an angel with a flaming sword; that would be easier for a sinning heart . . . instead of which he had himself to plunge the knife in. . . . Infamous! But to turn back, to abandon that other, to take advantage of the freedom offered him, recognised as his. . . . No! better to die! No, he would have none of such loathsome freedom . . . but would humble himself in the dust, and might those eyes look down on him with love. . . .

'Grigory Mihalitch,' said a melancholy voice, and some one's hand was laid heavily upon Litvinov.

He looked round in some alarm and recognised Potugin.

'I beg your pardon, Grigory Mihalitch,' began the latter with his customary humility, 'I am disturbing you perhaps, but, seeing you in the distance, I thought. . . . However if you're not in the humour. . . .'

'On the contrary I'm delighted,' Litvinov muttered between his teeth.

Potugin walked beside him.

'What a lovely evening!' he began, 'so warm! Have you been walking long?'

'No, not long.'

'Why do I ask though; I've just seen you come out of the *Hôtel de l'Europe.*'

'Then you've been following me?'

'Yes.'

'You have something to say to me?'

'Yes,' Potugin repeated, hardly audibly.

Litvinov stopped and looked at his uninvited companion. His face was pale, his eyes moved restlessly; his contorted features seemed overshadowed by old, long-standing grief.

'What do you specially want to say to me?' Litvinov said slowly, and he moved forward.

'Ah, with your permission . . . directly. If it's all the same to you, let us sit down here on this seat. It will be most convenient.'

'Why, this is something mysterious,' Litvinov declared, seating himself near him. 'You don't seem quite yourself, Sozont Ivanitch.'

'No; I'm all right; and it's nothing mysterious either. I specially wanted to tell you ... the impression made on me by your betrothed ... she is betrothed to you, I think? ... well, anyway, by the girl to whom you introduced me to-day. I must say that in the course of my whole existence I have never met a more attractive creature. A heart of gold, a really angelic nature.'

Potugin uttered all these words with the same bitter and mournful air, so that even Litvinov could not help noticing the incongruity between his expression of face and his speech.

'You have formed a perfectly correct estimate of Tatyana Petrovna,' Litvinov began, 'though I can't help being surprised, first that you should be aware of the relation in which I stand to her; and secondly, that you should have understood her so quickly. She really has an angelic nature; but allow me to ask, did you want to talk to me about this?'

'It's impossible not to understand her at once,' Potugin replied quickly, as though evading the last question. 'One need only take one look into her eyes. She deserves every possible happiness on earth, and enviable is the fate of the man whose lot it is to give her that happiness! One must hope he may prove worthy of such a fate.'

Litvinov frowned slightly.

'Excuse me, Sozont Ivanitch,' he said, 'I

must confess our conversation strikes me as altogether rather original. . . . I should like to know, does the hint contained in your words refer to me?'

Potugin did not at once answer Litvinov; he was visibly struggling with himself.

'Grigory Mihalitch,' he began at last, 'either I am completely mistaken in you, or you are capable of hearing the truth, from whomsoever it may come, and in however unattractive a form it may present itself. I told you just now, that I saw where you came from.'

'Why, from the *Hôtel de l'Europe*. What of that?'

'I know, of course, whom you have been to see there.'

'What?'

'You have been to see Madame Ratmirov.'

'Well, I have been to see her. What next?'

'What next? . . . You, betrothed to Tatyana Petrovna, have been to see Madame Ratmirov, whom you love . . . and who loves you.'

Litvinov instantly got up from the seat; the blood rushed to his head.

'What's this?' he cried at last, in a voice of concentrated exasperation: 'stupid jesting, spying? Kindly explain yourself.'

Potugin turned a weary look upon him.

'Ah! don't be offended at my words, Grigory

Mihalitch, me you cannot offend. I did not begin to talk to you for that, and I'm in no joking humour now.'

'Perhaps, perhaps. I'm ready to believe in the excellence of your intentions; but still I may be allowed to ask you by what right you meddle in the private affairs, in the inner life, of another man, a man who is nothing to you; and what grounds you have for so confidently giving out your own . . . invention for the truth?'

'My invention! If I had imagined it, it should not have made you angry; and as for my right, well I never heard before that a man ought to ask himself whether he had the right to hold out a hand to a drowning man.'

'I am humbly grateful for your tender solicitude,' cried Litvinov passionately, 'but I am not in the least in need of it, and all the phrases about the ruin of inexperienced young men wrought by society women, about the immorality of fashionable society, and so on, I look upon merely as stock phrases, and indeed in a sense I positively despise them; and so I beg you to spare your rescuing arm, and to let me drown in peace.'

Potugin again raised his eyes to Litvinov. He was breathing hard, his lips were twitching

'But look at me, young man,' broke from him

at last, and he clapped himself on the breast: 'can you suppose I have anything in common with the ordinary, self-satisfied moralist, a preacher? Don't you understand that simply from interest in you, however strong it might be, I would never have let fall a word, I would never have given you grounds for reproaching me with what I hate above all things—indiscretion, intrusiveness? Don't you see that this is something of a different kind altogether, that before you is a man crushed, utterly obliterated by the very passion, from the results of which he would save you, and . . . and for the same woman!'

Litvinov stepped back a pace.

'Is it possible? What did you say? . . . You . . . you . . . Sozont Ivanitch? But Madame Byelsky . . . that child?'

'Ah, don't cross-examine me . . . Believe me! That is a dark terrible story, and I'm not going to tell you it. Madame Byelsky I hardly knew, that child is not mine, but I took it all upon myself . . . because . . . *she* wished it, because it was necessary for *her*. Why am I here in your hateful Baden? And, in fact, could you suppose, could you for one instant imagine, that I'd have brought myself to caution you out of sympathy for you? I'm sorry for that sweet, good girl, your *fiancée*, but what have

I to do with your future, with you both? . . . But I am afraid for her . . . for her.'

'You do me great honour, Mr. Potugin,' began Litvinov, 'but since, according to you, we are both in the same position, why is it you don't apply such exhortations to yourself, and ought I not to ascribe your apprehensions to another feeling?'

'That is to jealousy, you mean? Ah, young man, young man, it's shameful of you to shuffle and make pretences, it's shameful of you not to realise what a bitter sorrow is speaking to you now by my lips! No, I am not in the same position as you! I, I am old, ridiculous, an utterly harmless old fool—but you! But there's no need to talk about it! You would not for one second agree to accept the position I fill, and fill with gratitude! Jealousy? A man is not jealous who has never had even a drop of hope, and this is not the first time it has been my lot to endure this feeling. I am only afraid . . . afraid for her, understand that. And could I have guessed when she sent me to you that the feeling of having wronged you—she owned to feeling that—would carry her so far?'

'But excuse me, Sozont Ivanitch, you seem to know . . .'

'I know nothing, and I know everything! I know,' he added, turning away, 'I know where she was yesterday. But there's no holding her back now; like a stone set rolling, she must roll on to the bottom. I should be a great idiot indeed, if I imagined my words could hold you back at once . . . you, when a woman like that . . . But that's enough of this. I couldn't restrain myself, that's my whole excuse. And after all how can one know, and why not try? Perhaps, you will think again; perhaps, some word of mine will go to your heart, you will not care to ruin her and yourself, and that innocent sweet creature . . . Ah! don't be angry, don't stamp about! What have I to fear? Why should I mince matters? It's not jealousy speaking in me, not anger . . . I'm ready to fall at your feet, to beseech you . . . Good-bye, though. You needn't be afraid, all this will be kept secret. I wished for your good.'

Potugin strode off along the avenue and quickly vanished in the now falling darkness. Litvinov did not detain him.

'A terrible dark story . . .' Potugin had said to Litvinov, and would not tell it . . . Let us pass it over with a few words only.

Eight years before, it had happened to him to be sent by his department to Count Reisenbach as a temporary clerk. It was in the summer. Potugin used to drive to his country villa with papers, and be whole days there at a time. Irina was then living at the count's. She was never haughty with people in a humbler station, at least she never treated them superciliously, and the countess more than once reproved her for her excessive Moscow familiarity. Irina soon detected a man of intelligence in the humble clerk, attired in the stiffly buttoned frockcoat that was his uniform. She used often and eagerly to talk to him . . . while he . . . he fell in love with her passionately, profoundly, secretly . . . Secretly! So *he* thought. The summer passed; the count no longer needed any outside assistance. Potugin lost sight of Irina but could not forget her. Three years after, he utterly unexpectedly received an invitation, through a third person, to go to see a lady slightly known to him. This lady at first was reluctant to speak out, but after exacting an oath from him to keep everything he was going to hear absolutely secret, she proposed to him . . . to marry a girl, who occupied a conspicuous position in society, and for whom marriage had become a necessity. The lady scarcely ventured to hint at the principal personage, and then promised Potugin money . . . a large sum of money. Potugin was not offended, astonishment stifled all feeling of anger in him; but, of course, he point-blank declined. Then the lady handed him a note—from Irina. 'You are a generous, noble man,' she wrote, 'and I know you would do anything for me; I beg of you this sacrifice. You will save one who is very dear to me. In saving her, you will save me too ... Do not ask me how. I could never have brought myself to any one with such an entreaty, but to you I hold out my hands and say to you, do it for my sake.' Potugin pondered, and said that for Irina Pavlovna, certainly he was ready to do a great deal; but he should like to hear her wishes from her own lips. The interview took place the same evening; it did not last long, and no one knew of it, except the same lady. Irina was no longer living at Count Reisenbach's.

'What made you think of me, of all people?' Potugin asked her.

She was beginning to expatiate on his noble qualities, but suddenly she stopped ...

'No,' she said, 'you must be told the truth. I know, I know that you love me; so that was why I made up my mind ...' and then she told him everything.

Eliza Byelsky was an orphan; her relations did not like her, and reckoned on her inheritance ... ruin was facing her. In saving her, Irina was really doing a service to him who was responsible for it all, and who was himself now standing in a very close relation to Irina . . . Potugin, without speaking, looked long at Irina, and consented. She wept, and flung herself all in tears on his neck. And he too wept . . . but very different were their tears. Everything had already been made ready for the secret marriage, a powerful hand removed all obstacles. . . . But illness came . . . and then a daughter was born, and then the mother . . . poisoned herself. What was to be done with the child? Potugin received it into his charge, received it from the same hands, from the hands of Irina.

A terrible dark story . . . Let us pass on, readers, pass on!

Over an hour more passed before Litvinov could bring himself to go back to his hotel. He had almost reached it when he suddenly heard steps behind him. It seemed as though they were following him persistently, and walking faster when he quickened his pace. When he moved under a lamp-post Litvinov turned round and recognised General Ratmirov. In a white tie, in a fashionable overcoat, flung open, with a row of stars and crosses on a golden chain in the buttonhole of his dresscoat, the general was returning from dinner, alone. His eyes, fastened with insolent persistence on Litvinov, expressed such contempt and such hatred, his whole deportment was suggestive of such intense defiance, that Litvinov thought it his duty, stifling his wrath, to go to meet him, to face a 'scandal.' But when he was on a level with Litvinov, the general's face suddenly changed, his habitual playful refinement reappeared upon it, and his hand in its pale lavender glove flourished his glossy hat high in the air. Litvinov took off his in silence, and each went on his way.

'He has noticed something, for certain!' thought Litvinov.

'If only it were . . . any one else!' thought the general.

Tatyana was playing picquet with her aunt when Litvinov entered their room.

'Well, I must say, you're a pretty fellow!' cried Kapitolina Markovna, and she threw down her cards. 'Our first day, and he's lost for the whole evening! Here we've been waiting and waiting, and scolding and scolding . . .'

'I said nothing, aunt,' observed Tatyana.

'Well, you're meekness itself, we all know! You ought to be ashamed, sir! and you betrothed too!'

Litvinov made some sort of excuse and sat down to the table.

'Why have you left off your game?' he asked after a brief silence.

'Well, that's a nice question! We've been

playing cards from sheer dulness, not knowing what to do with ourselves . . . but now you've come.'

'If you would care to hear the evening music,' observed Litvinov, 'I should be delighted to take you.'

Kapitolina Markovna looked at her niece.

'Let us go, aunt, I am ready,' she said, 'but wouldn't it be better to stay at home?'

'To be sure! Let us have tea in our own old Moscow way, with the samovar, and have a good chat. We've not had a proper gossip yet.'

Litvinov ordered tea to be sent up, but the good chat did not come off. He felt a continual gnawing of conscience; whatever he said, it always seemed to him that he was telling lies and Tatyana was seeing through it. Meanwhile there was no change to be observed in her; she behaved just as unconstrainedly . . . only her look never once rested upon Litvinov, but with a kind of indulgent timorousness glided over him, and she was paler than usual.

Kapitolina Markovna asked her whether she had not a headache.

Tatyana was at first about to say no, but after a moment's thought, she said, 'Yes, a little'

'It's the journey,' suggested Litvinov, and he positively blushed with shame.

'Yes, the journey,' repeated Tatyana, and her eyes again glided over him.

'You ought to rest, Tanya darling.'

'Yes, I will go to bed soon, aunt.'

On the table lay a *Guide des Voyageurs*; Litvinov fell to reading aloud the description of the environs of Baden.

'Quite so,' Kapitolina Markovna interrupted, ' but there's something we mustn't forget. I'm told linen is very cheap here, so we must be sure to buy some for the trousseau.'

Tatyana dropped her eyes.

We have plenty of time, aunt. You never think of yourself, but you really ought to get yourself some clothes. You see how smart every one is here.'

'Eh, my love! what would be the good of that? I'm not a fine lady! It would be another thing if I were such a beauty as your friend, Grigory Mihalitch, what was her name?'

'What friend?'

'Why, that we met to-day.'

'Oh, she!' said Litvinov, with feigned indifference, and again he felt disgust and shame. 'No!' he thought, 'to go on like this is impossible.'

He was sitting by his betrothed, while a few

inches from her in his side pocket, was Irina's handkerchief.

Kapitolina Markovna went for a minute into the other room.

'Tanya . . .' said Litvinov, with an effort. It was the first time that day he had called her by that name.

She turned towards him.

'I . . . I have something very important to say to you.'

'Oh! really? when? directly?'

'No, to-morrow.'

'Oh! to-morrow. Very well.'

Litvinov's soul was suddenly filled with boundless pity. He took Tatyana's hand and kissed it humbly, like a sinner; her heart throbbed faintly and she felt no happiness.

In the night, at two o'clock, Kapitolina Markovna, who was sleeping in the same room with her niece, suddenly lifted up her head and listened.

'Tanya,' she said, 'you are crying?'

Tatyana did not at once answer.

'No, aunt,' sounded her gentle voice, 'I've caught a cold.'

XX

'Why did I say that to her?' Litvinov thought the next morning as he sat in his room at the window. He shrugged his shoulders in vexation: he had said that to Tatyana simply to cut himself off all way of retreat. In the window lay a note from Irina: she asked him to see her at twelve. Potugin's words incessantly recurred to his mind, they seemed to reach him with a faint ill-omened sound as of a rumbling underground. He was angry with himself, but could not get rid of them anyhow. Some one knocked at the door.

'*Wer da?*' asked Litvinov.

'Ah! you're at home! open!' he heard Bindasov's hoarse bass.

The door handle creaked.

Litvinov turned white with exasperation.

'I'm not at home,' he declared sharply.

'Not at home? That's a good joke!'

'I tell you—not at home, get along.'

'That's civil! And I came to ask you for a little loan,' grumbled Bindasov.

He walked off, however, tramping on his heels as usual.

Litvinov was all but dashing out after him, he felt such a longing to throttle the hateful ruffian. The events of the last few days had unstrung his nerves; a little more, and he would have burst into tears. He drank off a glass of cold water, locked up all the drawers in the furniture, he could not have said why, and went to Tatyana's.

He found her alone. Kapitolina Markovna had gone out shopping. Tatyana was sitting on the sofa, holding a book in both hands. She was not reading it, and scarcely knew what book it was. She did not stir, but her heart was beating quickly in her bosom, and the little white collar round her neck quivered visibly and evenly.

Litvinov was confused. . . . However, he sat down by her, said good-morning, smiled at her; she too smiled at him without speaking. She had bowed to him when he came in, bowed courteously, not affectionately, and she did not glance at him. He held out his hand to her; she gave him her chill fingers, but at once freed them again, and took up the book. Litvinov felt that to begin the conversation with unimportant subjects would be insulting Tatyana; she after her custom made no demands, but everything in her said plainly, 'I am waiting, I am waiting.' . . . He must fulfil his promise. But though almost the whole night he had thought of nothing else, he had not prepared even the first introductory words, and absolutely did not know in what way to break this cruel silence.

'Tanya,' he began at last, 'I told you yesterday that I have something important to say to you. I am ready, only I beg you beforehand not to be angry against me, and to rest assured that my feelings for you . . .'

He stopped. He caught his breath. Tatyana still did not stir, and did not look at him; she only clutched the book tighter than ever.

'There has always been,' Litvinov went on, without finishing the sentence he had begun, 'there has always been perfect openness between us; I respect you too much to be a hypocrite with you; I want to prove to you that I know how to value the nobleness and independence of your nature, even though . . . though of course . . .'

'Grigory Mihalitch,' began Tatyana in a measured voice while a deathly pallor overspread her whole face, 'I will come to your ssistance, you no longer love me, and you don't know how to tell me so.'

Litvinov involuntarily shuddered.

'Why?' ... he said, hardly intelligibly, 'why could you suppose?... I really don't understand ...'

'What! isn't it the truth? Isn't it the truth? —tell me, tell me.'

Tatyana turned quite round to Litvinov; her face, with her hair brushed back from it, approached his face, and her eyes, which for so long had not looked at him, seemed to penetrate into his eyes.

'Isn't it the truth?' she repeated.

He said nothing, did not utter a single sound. He could not have lied at that instant, even if he had known she would believe him, and that his lie would save her; he was not even able to bear her eyes upon him. Litvinov said nothing, but she needed no answer, she read the answer in his very silence, in those guilty downcast eyes—and she turned away again and dropped the book.... She had been still uncertain till that instant, and Litvinov understood that; he understood that she had been still uncertain—and how hideous, actually hideous was all that he was doing.

He flung himself on his knees before her.

'Tanya,' he cried, 'if only you knew how

hard it is for me to see you in this position, how awful to me to think that it's I ... I! My heart is torn to pieces, I don't know myself, I have lost myself, and you, and everything ... Everything is shattered, Tanya, everything! Could I dream that I ... I should bring such a blow upon you, my best friend, my guardian angel? ... Could I dream that we should meet like this, should spend such a day as yesterday! ...'

Tatyana was trying to get up and go away. He held her back by the border of her dress.

'No, listen to me a minute longer. You see I am on my knees before you, but I have not come to beg your forgiveness; you cannot, you ought not to forgive me. I have come to tell you that your friend is ruined, that he is falling into the pit, and would not drag you down with him. ... But save me ... no! even you cannot save me. I should push you away, I am ruined, Tanya, I am ruined past all help.'

Tatyana looked at Litvinov.

'You are ruined?' she said, as though not fully understanding him. 'You are ruined?'

'Yes, Tanya, I am ruined. All the past, all that was precious, everything I have lived for up till now, is ruined for me; everything is wretched, everything is shattered, and I don't know what awaits me in the future. You said

just now that I no longer loved you. ....
No, Tanya, I have not ceased to love you, but
a different, terrible, irresistible passion has come
upon me, has overborne me. I fought against
it while I could. . . .'

Tatyana got up, her brows twitched, her pale face darkened. Litvinov too rose to his feet.

'You love another woman,' she began, 'and I guess who she is. . . . We met her yesterday, didn't we? . . . Well, I see what is left for me to do now. Since you say yourself this passion is unalterable' . . . (Tatyana paused an instant, possibly she had still hoped Litvinov would not let this last word pass unchallenged, but he said nothing), 'it only remains for me to give you back . . . your word.'

Litvinov bent his head, as though submissively receiving a well-deserved blow.

'You have every right to be angry with me,' he said. 'You have every right to reproach me for feebleness . . . for deceit.'

Tatyana looked at him again.

'I have not reproached you, Litvinov, I don't blame you. I agree with you: the bitterest truth is better than what went on yesterday. What sort of a life could ours have been now!'

'What sort of a life will mine be now!' echoed mournfully in Litvinov's soul.

Tatyana went towards the door of the bedroom.

'I will ask you to leave me alone for a little time, Grigory Mihalitch—we will see each other again, we will talk again. All this has been so unexpected I want to collect myself a little . . . leave me alone . . . spare my pride. We shall see each other again.'

And uttering these words, Tatyana hurriedly withdrew and locked the door after her.

Litvinov went out into the street like a man dazed and stunned; in the very depths of his heart something dark and bitter lay hid, such a sensation must a man feel who has murdered another; and at the same time he felt easier as though he had at last flung off a hated load. Tatyana's magnanimity had crushed him, he felt vividly all that he had lost . . . and yet? with his regret was mingled irritation; he yearned towards Irina as to the sole refuge left him, and felt bitter against her. For some time Litvinov's feelings had been every day growing more violent and more complex; this complexity tortured him, exasperated him, he was lost in this chaos. He thirsted for one thing; to get out at last on to the path, whatever it might be, if only not to wander longer in this incomprehensible half-darkness. Practical people of Litvinov's sort ought never to be carried away by passion, it destroys the very meaning of their lives. . . . But nature cares nothing for logic, our human logic; she has her own, which we do not recognise and do not acknowledge till we are crushed under its wheel.

On parting from Tatyana, Litvinov held one thought in his mind, to see Irina; he set off indeed to see her. But the general was at home, so at least the porter told him, and he did not care to go in, he did not feel himself capable of hypocrisy, and he moved slowly off towards the Konversation Hall. Litvinov's incapacity for hypocrisy was evident that day to both Voroshilov and Pishtchalkin, who happened to meet him; he simply blurted out to the former that he was empty as a drum; to the latter that he bored every one to extinction; it was lucky indeed that Bindasov did come across him; there would certainly have been a '*grosser Scandal.*' Both the young men were stupefied; Voroshilov went so far as to ask himself whether his honour as an officer did not demand satisfaction? But like Gogol's lieutenant, Pirogov, he calmed himself with bread and butter in a café. Litvinov caught sight in the distance of Kapitolina Markovna running busily from shop to shop in her striped mantle. . . . He felt ashamed to face the good, absurd, generous old lady. Then he recalled

Potugin, their conversation yesterday. . . . Then something was wafted to him, something intangible and unmistakable : if a falling shadow shed a fragrance, it could not be more elusive, but he felt at once that it was Irina near him, and in fact she appeared a few paces from him, arm-in-arm with another lady ; their eyes met at once. Irina probably noticed something peculiar in the expression of Litvinov's face ; she stopped before a shop, in which a number of tiny wooden clocks of Black Forest make were exhibited, and summoning him by a motion of her head, she pointed to one of these clocks, and calling upon him to admire a charming clock-face with a painted cuckoo above it, she said, not in a whisper, but as though finishing a phrase begun, in her ordinary tone of voice, much less likely to attract the attention of outsiders, 'Come in an hour's time, I shall be alone.'

But at this moment the renowned lady-killer Monsieur Verdier swooped down upon her, and began to fall into ecstasies over the colour, *feuille morte*, of her gown and the low-crowned Spanish hat she wore tilted almost down to her eyebrows. . . Litvinov vanished in the crowd.

XXI

'GRIGORY,' Irina was saying to him two hours later, as she sat beside him on the sofa, and laid both hands on his shoulder, 'what is the matter with you? Tell me now quickly, while we're alone.'

'The matter with me?' said Litvinov. 'I am happy, happy, that's what's the matter with me.'

Irina looked down, smiled, sighed.

'That's not an answer to my question, my dear one.'

Litvinov grew thoughtful.

'Well, let me tell you then . . . since you insist positively on it' (Irina opened her eyes wide and trembled slightly), 'I have told everything to-day to my betrothed.'

'What, everything? You mentioned me?'

Litvinov fairly threw up his arms.

'Irina, for God's sake, how could such an idea enter your head! that I——'

'There, forgive me . . . forgive me. What did you say?'

'I told her that I no longer loved her.'

'She asked why?'

'I did not disguise the fact that I loved another woman, and that we must part.'

'Ah . . . and what did she do? Agreed?'

'O Irina! what a girl she is! She was all self-sacrifice, all generosity!'

'I've no doubt, I've no doubt . . . there was nothing else for her to do, though.'

'And not one reproach, not one hard word to me, who have spoiled her whole life, deceived her, pitilessly flung her over. . . .'

Irina scrutinised her finger nails.

'Tell me, Grigory . . . did she love you?'

'Yes, Irina, she loved me.'

Irina was silent a minute, she straightened her dress.

'I must confess,' she began, 'I don't quite understand what induced you to explain matters to her.'

'What induced me, Irina! Would you have liked me to lie, to be a hypocrite to her, that pure soul? or did you suppose——'

'I supposed nothing,' Irina interrupted. 'I must admit I have thought very little about her. I don't know how to think of two people at once.'

'That is, you mean——'

'Well, and so what then? Is she going

away, that pure soul?' Irina interrupted a second time.

'I know nothing,' answered Litvinov. 'I am to see her again. But she will not stay.'

'Ah! *bon voyage!*'

'No, she will not stay. But I'm not thinking of her either now, I am thinking of what you said to me, what you have promised me.'

Irina looked up at him from under her eyelids.

'Ungrateful one! aren't you content yet?'

'No, Irina, I'm not content. You have made me happy, but I'm not content, and you understand me.'

'That is, I——'

'Yes, you understand me. Remember your words, remember what you wrote to me. I can't share you with others; no, no, I can't consent to the pitiful rôle of secret lover; not my life alone, this other life too I have flung at your feet, I have renounced everything, I have crushed it all to dust, without compunction and beyond recall; but in return I trust, I firmly believe, that you too will keep your promise, and unite your lot with mine for ever.'

'You want me to run away with you? I am ready....' (Litvinov bent down to her hands in ecstasy.) 'I am ready. I will not go back from my word. But have you yourself thought over all the difficulties—have you made preparations?'

'I? I have not had time yet to think over or prepare anything, but only say yes, let me act, and before a month is over . . .'

'A month! we start for Italy in a fortnight.'

'A fortnight, then, is enough for me. O Irina, you seem to take my proposition coldly; perhaps it seems unpractical to you, but I am not a boy, I am not used to comforting myself with dreams, I know what a tremendous step this is, I know what a responsibility I am taking on myself; but I can see no other course. Think of it, I must break every tie with the past, if only not to be a contemptible liar in the eyes of the girl I have sacrificed for you!'

Irina drew herself up suddenly and her eyes flashed.

'Oh, I beg your pardon, Grigory Mihalitch! If I decide, if I run away, then it will at least be with a man who does it for my sake, for my sake simply, and not in order that he may not degrade himself in the good opinion of a phlegmatic young person, with milk and water, *du lait coupé* instead of blood, in her veins! And I must tell you too, it's the first time, I confess, that it's been my lot to hear that the man I honour with my regard is deserving of commiseration, playing a pitiful part! I know a far more pitiful part, the part of a man who doesn't know what is going on in his own heart!'

Litvinov drew himself up in his turn.

'Irina,' he was beginning——

But all at once she clapped both hands to her forehead, and with a convulsive motion, flinging herself on his breast, she embraced him with force beyond a woman's.

'Forgive me, forgive me,' she began, with a shaking voice, 'forgive me, Grigory! You see how corrupted I am, how horrid I am, how jealous and wicked! You see how I need your aid, your indulgence! Yes, save me, drag me out of this mire, before I am quite ruined! Yes, let us run away, let us run away from these people, from this society to some far off, fair, free country! Perhaps your Irina will at last be worthier of the sacrifices you are making for her! Don't be angry with me, forgive me, my sweet, and know that I will do everything you command, I will go anywhere you will take me!'

Litvinov's heart was in a turmoil. Irina clung closer than before to him with all her youthful supple body. He bent over her fragrant, disordered tresses, and in an intoxication of gratitude and ecstasy, he hardly dared to caress them with his hand, he hardly touched them with his lips.

'Irina, Irina,' he repeated,—'my angel....'

She suddenly raised her head, listened....

'It's my husband's step, ... he has gone into his room,' she whispered, and, moving hurriedly away, she crossed over to another armchair. Litvinov was getting up.... 'What are you doing?' she went on in the same whisper; 'you must stay, he suspects you as it is. Or are you afraid of him?' She did not take her eyes off the door. 'Yes, it's he; he will come in here directly. Tell me something, talk to me.' Litvinov could not at once recover himself and was silent. 'Aren't you going to the theatre to-morrow?' she uttered aloud. 'They're giving *Le Verre d'Eau*, an old-fashioned piece, and Plessy is awfully affected.... We're as though we were in a perfect fever,' she added, dropping her voice. 'We can't do anything like this; we must think things over well. I ought to warn you that all my money is in his hands; *mais j'ai mes bijoux*. We'll go to Spain, would you like that?' She raised her voice again. 'Why is it all actresses get so fat? Madeleine Brohan for instance.... Do talk, don't sit so silent. My head is going round. But you, you must not doubt me.... I will let you know where to come to-morrow. Only it was a mistake to have told that young lady.... *Ah, mais c'est charmant!*' she cried suddenly and with a nervous laugh, she tore the lace edge of her handkerchief.

'May I come in?' asked Ratmirov from the other room.

'Yes . . . yes.'

The door opened, and in the doorway appeared the general. He scowled on seeing Litvinov; however, he bowed to them, that is to say, he bent the upper portion of his person.

'I did not know **you** had a visitor,' he said: '*je vous demande pardon de mon indiscrétion.* So you still find Baden entertaining, M'sieu—Litvinov?'

Ratmirov always uttered Litvinov's surname with hesitation, every time, as though he had forgotten it, and could not at once recall it. . . . In this way, as well as by the lofty flourish of his hat in saluting him, he meant to insult his pride.

'I am not bored here, *m'sieu le général.*'

'Really? Well, I find Baden fearfully boring. We are soon going away, are we not, Irina Pavlovna? *Assez de Bade comme ça.* By the way, I've won you five hundred francs to-day.'

Irina stretched out her hand coquettishly.

'Where are they? Please let me have them for pin-money.'

'You shall have them, you shall have them. . . . You are going, M'sieu—Litvinov?'

'Yes, I am going, as you see.'

Ratmirov again bent his body.

'Till we meet again!'

'Good-bye, Grigory Mihalitch,' said Irina. 'I will keep my promise.'

'What is that? May I be inquisitive?' her husband queried.

Irina smiled.

'No, it was only . . . something we've been talking of. *C'est à propos du voyage . . . où il vous plaira.* You know—Stael's book?'

'Ah! ah! to be sure, I know. Charming illustrations.'

Ratmirov seemed on the best of terms with his wife; he called her by her pet name in addressing her.

XXII

'BETTER not think now, really,' Litvinov repeated, as he strode along the street, feeling that the inward riot was rising up again in him. 'The thing's decided. She will keep her promise, and it only remains for me to take all necessary steps. . . . Yet she hesitates, it seems.' . . . He shook his head. His own designs struck even his own imagination in a strange light; there was a smack of artificiality, of unreality about them. One cannot dwell long upon the same thoughts; they gradually shift like the bits of glass in a kaleidoscope . . . one peeps in, and already the shapes before one's eyes are utterly different. A sensation of intense weariness overcame Litvinov. . . . If he could for one short hour but rest! . . . But Tanya? He started, and, without reflecting even, turned submissively homewards, merely struck by the idea, that this day was tossing him like a ball from one to the other. . . . No matter; he must make an end. He went back to his hotel, and with the same submissiveness, insensibility, numbness, without hesitation or delay, he went to see Tatyana.

He was met by Kapitolina Markovna. From the first glance at her, he knew that she knew about it all; the poor maiden lady's eyes were swollen with weeping, and her flushed face, fringed with her dishevelled white locks, expressed dismay and an agony of indignation, sorrow, and boundless amazement. She was on the point of rushing up to Litvinov, but she stopped short, and, biting her quivering lip, she looked at him as though she would supplicate him, and kill him, and assure herself that it was a dream, a senseless, impossible thing, wasn't it?

'Here you . . . you are come,' she began. . . . The door from the next room opened instantaneously, and with a light tread Tatyana came in; she was of a transparent pallor, but she was quite calm.

She gently put one arm round her aunt and made her sit down beside her.

'You sit down too, Grigory Mihalitch,' she said to Litvinov, who was standing like one distraught at the door. 'I am very glad to see you once more. I have informed auntie of your decision, our common decision; she fully shares it and approves of it. . . . Without mutual love there can be no happiness, mutual esteem alone is not enough' (at the word 'esteem' Litvinov involuntarily looked down) 'and better to separate now, than to repent later. Isn't it, aunt?'

'Yes, of course,' began Kapitolina Markovna, 'of course, Tanya darling, the man who does not know how to appreciate you . . . who could bring himself——'

'Aunt, aunt,' Tatyana interrupted, 'remember what you promised me. You always told me yourself: truth, Tatyana, truth before everything—and independence. Well, truth's not always sweet, nor independence either; or else where would be the virtue of it?'

She kissed Kapitolina Markovna on her white hair, and turning to Litvinov, she went on:

'We propose, aunt and I, leaving Baden.... I think it will be more comfortable so for all of us.'

'When do you think of going?' Litvinov said thickly. He remembered that Irina had said the very same words to him not long before.

Kapitolina Markovna was darting forward, but Tatyana held her back, with a caressing touch on her shoulder.

'Probably soon, very soon.'

'And will you allow me to ask where you

intend going?' Litvinov said in the same voice.

'First to Dresden, then probably to Russia.'

'But what can you want to know that for now, Grigory Mihalitch?' . . . cried Kapitolina Markovna.

'Aunt, aunt,' Tatyana interposed again. A brief silence followed.

'Tatyana Petrovna,' began Litvinov, 'you know how agonisingly painful and bitter my feelings must be at this instant.'

Tatyana got up.

'Grigory Mihalitch,' she said, 'we will not talk about that . . . if you please, I beg you for my sake, if not for your own. I have known you long enough, and I can very well imagine what you must be feeling now. But what's the use of talking, of touching a sore' (she stopped; it was clear she wanted to stem the emotion rushing upon her, to swallow the rising tears; she succeeded)—'why fret a sore we cannot heal? Leave that to time. And now I have to ask a service of you, Grigory Mihalitch; if you will be so good, I will give you a letter directly: take it to the post yourself, it is rather important, but aunt and I have no time now. . . . I shall be much obliged to you. Wait a minute. . . . I will bring it directly. . . .'

In the doorway Tatyana glanced uneasily at

Kapitolina Markovna; but she was sitting with such dignity and decorum, with such a severe expression on her knitted brows and tightly compressed lips, that Tatyana merely gave her a significant nod and went out.

But scarcely had the door closed behind her, when every trace of dignity and severity instantaneously vanished from Kapitolina Markovna's face; she got up, ran on tiptoe up to Litvinov, and all hunched together and trying to look him in the face, she began in a quaking tearful whisper:

'Good God,' she said, 'Grigory Mihalitch, what does it mean? is it a dream or what? *You* give up Tanya, you tired of her, you breaking your word! You doing this, Grigory Mihalitch, you on whom we all counted as if you were a stone wall! You? you? you, Grisha?' ... Kapitolina Markovna stopped. 'Why, you will kill her, Grigory Mihalitch,' she went on, without waiting for an answer, while her tears fairly coursed in fine drops over her cheeks. 'You mustn't judge by her bearing up now, you know her character! She never complains; she does not think of herself, so others must think of her! She keeps saying to me, "Aunt, we must save our dignity!" but what's dignity, when I foresee death, death before us?' ... Tatyana's chair creaked in the next room 'Yes, I foresee death,' the old lady went on still more softly. 'And how can such a thing have come about? Is it witchcraft, or what? It's not long since you were writing her the tenderest letters. And in fact can an honest man act like this? I'm a woman, free, as you know, from prejudice of any sort, *esprit fort*, and I have given Tanya too the same sort of education, she too has a free mind. . . .'

'Aunt!' came Tatyana's voice from the next room.

'But one's word of honour is a duty, Grigory Mihalitch, especially for people of your, of my principles! If we're not going to recognise duty, what is left us? This cannot be broken off in this way, at your whim, without regard to what may happen to another! It's unprincipled . . . yes, it's a crime; a strange sort of freedom!'

'Aunt, come here please,' was heard again.

'I'm coming, my love, I'm coming . . .' Kapitolina Markovna clutched at Litvinov's hand.—'I see you are angry, Grigory Mihalitch.' . . . ('Me! me angry?' he wanted to exclaim, but his tongue was dumb.) 'I don't want to make you angry—oh, really, quite the contrary! I've come even to entreat you; think again while there is time; don't destroy her, don't destroy your own happiness, she will still trust you, Grisha, she will believe in you, nothing is lost yet; why, she loves you as no one will ever love you! Leave this hateful Baden-Baden, let us go away together, only throw off this enchantment, and, above all, have pity, have pity———'

'Aunt!' called Tatyana, with a shade of impatience in her voice.

But Kapitolina Markovna did not hear her.

'Only say "yes,"' she repeated to Litvinov; 'and I will still make everything smooth. . . . You need only nod your head to me, just one little nod like this.'

Litvinov would gladly, he felt, have died at that instant; but the word 'yes' he did not utter, and he did not nod his head.

Tatyana reappeared with a letter in her hand. Kapitolina Markovna at once darted away from Litvinov, and, averting her face, bent low over the table, as though she were looking over the bills and papers that lay on it.

Tatyana went up to Litvinov.

'Here,' she said, 'is the letter I spoke of. . . . You will go to the post at once with it, won't you?'

Litvinov raised his eyes. . . . Before him, really, stood his judge. Tatyana struck him as taller, slenderer; her face, shining with unwonted beauty, had the stony grandeur of a statue's; her bosom did not heave, and her gown, of one colour and straight as a Greek chiton, fell in the long, unbroken folds of marble drapery to her feet, which were hidden by it. Tatyana was looking straight before her, only at Litvinov; her cold, calm gaze, too, was the gaze of a statue. He read his sentence in it; he bowed, took a letter from the hand held out so immovably to him, and silently withdrew.

Kapitolina Markovna ran to Tatyana; but the latter turned off her embraces and dropped her eyes; a flush of colour spread over her face, and with the words, 'and now, the sooner the better,' she went into the bedroom. Kapitolina Markovna followed her with hanging head.

The letter, entrusted to Litvinov by Tatyana, was addressed to one of her Dresden friends—a German lady—who let small furnished apartments. Litvinov dropped the letter into the post-box, and it seemed to him as though with that tiny scrap of paper he was dropping all his past, all his life into the tomb. He went out of the town, and strolled a long time by narrow paths between vineyards; he could not shake off the persistent sensation of contempt for himself, like the importunate buzzing of flies in summer: an unenviable part, indeed, he had played in the last interview. . . . And when he went back to his hotel, and after a little time inquired about the ladies, he was told that immediately after he had gone out, they had given orders to be driven to the railway station, and had departed by the mail train—to what destination was not known. Their things had been packed and their bills paid ever since the morning. Tatyana had asked Litvinov to take her letter to the post, obviously with the object of getting him out of the way. He ventured to ask the hall-porter whether the ladies had left any letters for him, but the porter replied in the negative, and looked amazed even; it was clear that this sudden exit from rooms taken for a week struck him too as strange and dubious. Litvinov turned his back on him, and locked himself up in his room.

He did not leave it till the following day: the greater part of the night he was sitting at the table, writing, and tearing what he had written. . . The dawn was already beginning when he finished his task—it was a letter to Irina.

XXIII

THIS was what was in this letter to Irina:

'My betrothed went away yesterday; we shall never see each other again. . . . I do not know even for certain where she is going to live. With her, she takes all that till now seemed precious and desirable to me; all my previous ideas, my plans, my intentions, have gone with her; my labours even are wasted, my work of years ends in nothing, all my pursuits have no meaning, no applicability; all that is dead; myself, my old self, is dead and buried since yesterday. I feel, I see, I know this clearly . . . far am I from regretting this. Not to lament of it, have I begun upon this to you. . . . As though I could complain when you love me, Irina! I wanted only to tell you that, of all this dead past, all those hopes and efforts, turned to smoke and ashes, there is only one thing left living, invincible, my love for you. Except that love, nothing is left for me; to say it is the sole thing precious to me, would be too little; I live wholly in that love; that love is my whole being; in it are my future, my career, my vocation, my country! You know me, Irina; you know that fine talk of any sort is foreign to my nature, hateful to me, and however strong the words in which I try to express my feelings, you will have no doubts of their sincerity, you will not suppose them exaggerated. I'm not a boy, in the impulse of momentary ecstasy, lisping unreflecting vows to you, but a man of matured age—simply and plainly, almost with terror, telling you what he has recognised for unmistakable truth. Yes, your love has replaced everything for me — everything, everything! Judge for yourself: can I leave this my *all* in the hands of another? can I let him dispose of you? You—you will belong to him, my whole being, my heart's blood will belong to him—while I myself ... where am I? what am I? An outsider—an onlooker ... looking on at my own life! No, that's impossible, impossible! To share, to share in secret that without which it's useless, impossible to live ... that's deceit and death. I know how great a sacrifice I am asking of you, without any sort of right to it; indeed, what can give one a right to sacrifice? But I am not acting thus from egoism: an egoist would find it easier and smoother not to raise this question at all. Yes, my demands are difficult, and I am not surprised that they alarm you. The people among whom you have to live are hateful to you, you are sick of society, but are you strong enough to throw up that society? to trample on the success it has crowned you with? to rouse public opinion against you—the opinion of these hateful people? Ask yourself, Irina, don't take a burden upon you greater than you can bear. I don't want to reproach you; but remember: once already you could not hold out against temptation. I can give you so little in return for all you are losing. Hear my last word: if you don't feel capable to-morrow, to-day even, of leaving all and following me—you see how boldly I speak, how little I spare myself,— if you are frightened at the uncertainty of the future, and estrangement and solitude and the censure of men, if you cannot rely on yourself, in fact, tell me so openly and without delay, and I will go away; I shall go with a broken heart, but I shall bless you for your truthfulness. But if you really, my beautiful, radiant queen, love a man so petty, so obscure as I, and are really ready to share his fate,—well, then, give me your hand, and let us set off together on our difficult way! Only understand, my decision is unchanging; either all or nothing it's unreasonable . . . but I could not do otherwise—I cannot, Irina! I love you too much.—Yours,   G. L.'

Litvinov did not much like this letter himself; it did not quite truly and exactly express what he wanted to say; it was full of awkward expressions, high flown or bookish, and doubtless it was not better than many of the other letters he had torn up; but it was the last, the chief point was thoroughly stated anyway, and harassed, and worn out, Litvinov did not feel capable of dragging anything else out of his head. Besides he did not possess the faculty of putting his thought into literary form, and like all people with whom it is not habitual, he took great trouble over the style. His first letter was probably the best; it came warmer from the heart. However that might be, Litvinov despatched his missive to Irina.

She replied in a brief note:

'Come to me to-day,' she wrote to him: '*he* has gone away for the whole day. Your letter has greatly disturbed me. I keep thinking, thinking . . . and my head is in a whirl. I am very wretched, but you love me, and I am happy. Come. Yours,   I.'

She was sitting in her boudoir when Litvinov went in. He was conducted there by the same little girl of thirteen who on the previous day had watched for him on the stairs. On the table before Irina was standing an open, semicircular, cardboard box of lace: she was carelessly turning over the lace with one hand, in the other she was holding Litvinov's letter. She had only just left off crying; her eyelashes were wet, and her eyelids swollen; on her cheeks could be seen the traces of undried tears not wiped away. Litvinov stood still in the doorway; she did not notice his entrance.

'You are crying?' he said wonderingly.

She started, passed her hand over her hair and smiled.

'Why are you crying?' repeated Litvinov. She pointed in silence to the letter. 'So you were . . . over that,' he articulated haltingly.

'Come here, sit down,' she said, 'give me your hand. Well, yes, I was crying . . . what are you surprised at? Is that nothing?' she pointed again to the letter.

Litvinov sat down.

'I know it's not easy, Irina, I tell you so indeed in my letter . . . I understand your position. But if you believe in the value of your love for me, if my words have convinced you, you ought, too, to understand what I feel now at the sight of your tears. I have come here, like a man on his trial, and I await what is to be my sentence? Death or life? Your answer decides everything. Only don't look at me with those eyes. . . . They remind me of the eyes I saw in old days in Moscow.'

Irina flushed at once, and turned away, as though herself conscious of something evil in her gaze.

'Why do you say that, Grigory? For shame! You want to know my answer . . . do you mean to say you can doubt it? You are troubled by my tears . . . but you don't understand them. Your letter, dearest, has set me thinking. Here you write that my love has replaced everything for you, that even your former studies can never now be put into practice; but I ask myself, can a man live for love alone? Won't it weary him at last, won't he want an active career, and won't he cast the blame on what drew him away from active life? That's the thought that dismays me, that's what I am afraid of, and not what you imagine.'

Litvinov looked intently at Irina, and Irina intently looked at him, as though each would penetrate deeper and further into the soul of the other, deeper and further than word can reach, or word betray.

'You are wrong in being afraid of that,' began Litvinov. 'I must have expressed myself badly. Weariness? Inactivity? With the new impetus your love will give me? O Irina, in your love there's a whole world for me, and I can't yet foresee myself what may develop from it.'

Irina grew thoughtful.

'Where are we going?' she whispered.

'Where? We will talk of that later. But, of course, then ... then you agree? you agree, Irina?'

She looked at him. 'And you will be happy?'

'O Irina!'

'You will regret nothing? Never?'

She bent over the cardboard box, and again began looking over the lace in it.

'Don't be angry with me, dear one, for attending to this trash at such a moment. . . . I am obliged to go to a ball at a certain lady's, these bits of finery have been sent me, and I must choose to-day. Ah! I am awfully wretched!' she cried suddenly, and she laid her face down on the edge of the box. Tears began falling again from her eyes. . . . She turned away; the tears might spoil the lace.

'Irina, you are crying again,' Litvinov began uneasily.

'Ah, yes, again,' Irina interposed hurriedly. 'O Grigory, don't torture me, don't torture yourself! . . . Let us be free people! What does it matter if I do cry! And indeed do I know myself why my tears are flowing? You know, you have heard my decision, you believe it will not be changed. That I agree to . What was it you said? . . . to all or nothing . . . what more would you have? Let us be free! Why these mutual chains? We are alone together now, you love me. I love you; is it possible we have nothing to do but wringing our thoughts out of each other? Look at me, I don't want to talk about myself, I have never by one word hinted that for me perhaps it was not so easy to set at nought my duty as a wife . . . and, of course, I don't deceive myself, I know I am a criminal, and that *he* has a right to kill me. Well, what of it? Let us be free, I say. To-day is ours—a life-time's ours.'

She got up from the arm-chair and looked at Litvinov with her head thrown back, faintly smiling and moving her eyebrows, while with one arm bare to the elbow she pushed back from her face a long tress on which a few tears glistened. A rich scarf slipped from the table and fell on the floor at Irina's feet. She trampled contemptuously on it. 'Or don't you like me, to-day? Have I grown ugly since yesterday? Tell me, have you often seen a prettier hand? And this hair? Tell me, do you love me?'

She clasped him in both arms, held his head close to her bosom, her comb fell out with a ringing sound, and her falling hair wrapped him in a soft flood of fragrance.

XXIV

LITVINOV walked up and down his room in the hotel, his head bowed in thought. He had now to pass from theory to practice, to devise ways and means for flight, for moving to unknown countries. . . . But, strange to say, he was not pondering so much upon ways and means as upon whether actually, beyond doubt, the decision had been reached on which he had so obstinately insisted? Had the ultimate, irrevocable word been uttered? But Irina to be sure had said to him at parting, ' Act, act, and when every thing is ready, only let me know.' That was final! Away with all doubts. . . . He must proceed to action. And Litvinov proceeded —in the meantime—to calculation. Money first of all. Litvinov had, he found, in ready money one thousand three hundred and twenty-eight guldens, in French money, two thousand eight hundred and fifty-five francs; the sum was trifling, but it was enough for the first necessities, and then he must at once write to his father to send him all he could; he would have to sell the forest part of the land. But on what pretext? ... Well, a pretext would be found. Irina had spoken, it's true, of her *bijoux*, but that must not be taken into his reckoning; that, who knows, might come in for a rainy day. He had besides a good Geneva watch, for which he might get ... well, say, four hundred francs. Litvinov went to a banker's, and with much circumlocution introduced the question whether it was possible, in case of need, to borrow money; but bankers at Baden are wary old foxes, and in response to such circumlocutions they promptly assume a drooping and blighted air, for all the world like a wild flower whose stalk has been severed by the scythe; some indeed laugh outright in your face, as though appreciating an innocent joke on your part. Litvinov, to his shame, even tried his luck at roulette, even, oh ignominy! put a thaler on the number thirty, corresponding with his own age. He did this with a view to augmenting and rounding off his capital; and if he did not augment it, he certainly did round off his capital by losing the odd twenty-eight guldens. There was a second question, also not an unimportant one; that was the passport. But for a woman a passport is not quite so obligatory, and there are countries where it is not required at all, Belgium, for instance, and England; besides, one might even get some other passport, not Russian. Litvinov pondered very seriously on all this; his decision was firm, absolutely unwavering, and yet all the time against his will, overriding his will, something not serious, almost humorous came in, filtered through his musings, as though the very enterprise were a comic business, and no one ever did elope with any one in reality, but only in plays and novels, and perhaps somewhere in the provinces, in some of those remote districts, where, according to the statements of travellers, people are literally sick continually from *ennui*. At that point Litvinov recalled how an acquaintance of his, a retired cornet, Batsov, had eloped with a merchant's daughter in a staging sledge with bells and three horses, having as a preliminary measure made the parents drunk, and adopted the same precaution as well with the bride, and how, as it afterwards turned out, he was outwitted and within an ace of a thrashing into the bargain. Litvinov felt exceedingly irritated with himself for such inappropriate reminiscences, and then with the recollection of Tatyana, her sudden departure, all that grief and suffering and shame, he felt only too acutely that the affair he was arranging was deadly earnest, and how right he had been when he had told Irina that his honour even left no other course open. . . . And again at the mere name something of flame turned with sweet ache about his heart and died away again.

The tramp of horses' hoofs sounded behind him. . . . He moved aside. . . . Irina overtook him on horseback; beside her rode the stout general. She recognised Litvinov, nodded to him, and lashing her horse with a sidestroke of her whip, she put him into a gallop, and suddenly dashed away at headlong speed. Her dark veil fluttered in the wind. . . .

'*Pas si vite! Nom de Dieu! pas si vite!*' cried the general, and he too galloped after her

XXV

The next morning Litvinov had only just come home from seeing the banker, with whom he had had another conversation on the playful instability of our exchange, and the best means of sending money abroad, when the hotel porter handed him a letter. He recognised Irina's handwriting, and without breaking the seal—a presentiment of evil, Heaven knows why, was astir in him—he went into his room. This was what he read (the letter was in French):

'My dear one, I have been thinking all night of your plan.... I am not going to shuffle with you. You have been open with me, and I will be open with you; I *cannot* run away with you, I *have not the strength* to do it. I feel how I am wronging you; my second sin is greater than the first, I despise myself, my cowardice, I cover myself with reproaches, but I cannot change myself. In vain I tell myself that I have destroyed your happiness, that you have the right now to regard me as a frivolous flirt, that I myself drew you on, that I have given you solemn promises. . . . I am full of horror, of hatred for myself, but I can't do otherwise, I can't, I can't. I don't want to justify myself, I won't tell you I was carried away myself . . . all that's of no importance; but I want to tell you, and to say it again and yet again, I am yours, yours for ever, do with me as you will when you will, free from all obligation, from all responsibility! I am yours. . . . But run away, throw up everything . . . no! no! no! I besought you to save me, I hoped to wipe out everything, to burn up the past as in a fire . . . but I see there is no salvation for me; I see the poison has gone too deeply into me; I see one cannot breathe this atmosphere for years with impunity. I have long hesitated whether to write you this letter, I dread to think what decision you may come to, I trust only to your love for me. But I felt it would be dishonest on my part to hide the truth from you—especially as perhaps you have already begun to take the first steps for carrying out our project. Ah! it was lovely but impracticable. O my dear one, think me a weak, worthless woman, despise, but don't abandon me, don't abandon your Irina! . . . To leave this life I have not the courage, but live it without you I cannot either. We soon go back to Petersburg, come there, live there, we will find occupation for you, your labours in the past shall not be thrown away, you shall find good use for them . . . only live near me, only love me; such as I am, with all my weaknesses and my vices, and believe me, no heart will ever be so tenderly devoted to you as the heart of your Irina. Come soon to me, I shall not have an instant's peace until I see you.—Yours, yours, yours,   I.'

The blood beat like a sledge-hammer in Litvinov's head, then slowly and painfully sank to his heart, and was chill as a stone in it. He read through Irina's letter, and just as on that day at Moscow he fell in exhaustion on the sofa, and stayed there motionless. A dark abyss seemed suddenly to have opened on all sides of him, and he stared into this darkness in senseless despair. And so again, again deceit, no, worse than deceit, lying and baseness. . . . And life shattered, everything torn up by its roots utterly, and the sole thing which he could cling to—the last prop in fragments too! 'Come after us to Petersburg,' he repeated with a bitter inward laugh, 'we will find you occupation. . . . Find me a place as a head clerk, eh? and who are *we*? Here there's a hint of her past. Here we have the secret, hideous something I know nothing of, but which she has been trying to wipe out, to burn as in a fire. Here we have that world of intrigues, of secret relations, of shameful stories of Byelskys and Dolskys.... And what a future, what a lovely part awaiting me! To live close to her, visit her, share with her the morbid melancholy of the lady of fashion who is sick and weary of the world, but can't live outside its circle, be the friend of the house of course, of his Excellency . . . until . . . until the whim changes and the plebeian lover loses his piquancy, and is replaced by that fat general or Mr. Finikov—that's possible and pleasant, and I dare say useful. . . . She talks of a good use for my talents? . . . but the other project's impracticable, impracticable. . . . In Litvinov's soul rose, like sudden gusts of wind before a storm, momentary impulses of fury. . . . Every expression in Irina's letter roused his indignation, her very assertions of her unchanging feelings affronted him. 'She can't let it go like that,' he cried at last, 'I won't allow her to play with my life so mercilessly.'

Litvinov jumped up, snatched his hat. But what was he to do? Run to her? Answer her letter? He stopped short, and his hands fell.

'Yes; what was to be done?'

Had he not himself put this fatal choice to her? It had not turned out as he had wished . . . there was that risk about every choice. She had changed her mind, it was true; she herself had declared at first that she would throw up everything and follow him; that was true too; but she did not deny her guilt, she called herself a weak woman; she did not want to deceive him, she had been deceived in herself. . . . What answer could be made to that? At any rate she was not hypocritical, she was not deceiving him . . . she was open, remorselessly open. There was nothing forced her to speak out, nothing to prevent her from soothing him with promises, putting things off, and keeping it all in uncertainty till her departure . . . till her departure with her husband for Italy? But she had ruined his life, ruined two lives. . . . What of that?

But as regards Tatyana, she was not guilty; the guilt was his, his, Litvinov's alone, and he had no right to shake off the responsibility his own sin had laid with iron yoke upon him. . . . All this was so; but what was left him to do now?

Again he flung himself on the sofa and again in gloom, darkly, dimly, without trace, with devouring swiftness, the minutes raced past. . . .

'And why not obey her?' flashed through his brain. 'She loves me, she is mine, and in our very yearning towards each other, in this passion, which after so many years has burst upon us, and forced its way out with such violence, is there not something inevitable, irresistible, like a law of nature? Live in Petersburg . . . and shall I be the first to be put in such a position? And how could we be in safety together? . . .'

And he fell to musing, and Irina's shape, in the guise in which it was imprinted for ever in his late memories, softly rose before him. . . . But not for long. . . . He mastered himself, and with a fresh outburst of indignation drove away from him both those memories and that seductive image.

'You give me to drink from that golden cup,' he cried, 'but there is poison in the draught, and your white wings are besmirched with mire. . . . Away! Remain here with you after the way I . . . I drove away my betrothed . . . a deed of infamy, of infamy!' He wrung his hands with anguish, and another face with the stamp of suffering on its still features, with dumb reproach in its farewell eyes, rose from the depths. . . .

And for a long time Litvinov was in this agony still; for a long time, his tortured thought, like a man fever-stricken, tossed from side to side. ... He grew calm at last; at last he came to a decision. From the very first instant he had a presentiment of this decision; ... it had appeared to him at first like a distant, hardly perceptible point in the midst of the darkness and turmoil of his inward conflict; then it had begun to move nearer and nearer, till it ended by cutting with icy edge into his heart.

Litvinov once more dragged his box out of the corner, once more he packed all his things, without haste, even with a kind of stupid carefulness, rang for the waiter, paid his bill, and despatched to Irina a note in Russian to the following purport:

'I don't know whether you are doing me a greater wrong now than then; but I know this present blow is infinitely heavier. ... It is the end. You tell me, "I cannot"; and I repeat to you, "I cannot ..." do what you want. I cannot and I don't want to. Don't answer me. You are not capable of giving me the only answer I would accept. I am going away to-morrow early by the first train. Good-bye, may you be happy! We shall in all probability not see each other again.'

Till night-time Litvinov did not leave his room; God knows whether he was expecting anything. About seven o'clock in the evening a lady in a black mantle with a veil on her face twice approached the steps of his hotel. Moving a little aside and gazing far away into the distance, she suddenly made a resolute gesture with her hand, and for the third time went towards the steps. . . .

'Where are you going, Irina Pavlovna?' she heard a voice utter with effort behind her.

She turned with nervous swiftness. . . . Potugin ran up to her.

She stopped short, thought a moment, and fairly flung herself towards him, took his arm, and drew him away.

'Take me away, take me away,' she repeated breathlessly.

'What is it, Irina Pavlovna?' he muttered in bewilderment.

'Take me away,' she reiterated with redoubled force, 'if you don't want me to remain for ever . . . there.'

Potugin bent his head submissively, and hurriedly they went away together.

The following morning early Litvinov was perfectly ready for his journey—into his room walked . . . Potugin.

He went up to him in silence, and in silence shook his hand. Litvinov, too, said nothing. Both of them wore long faces, and both vainly tried to smile.

'I came to wish you a good journey,' Potugin brought out at last.

'And how did you know I was going to-day?' asked Litvinov.

Potugin looked on the floor around him . . . 'I became aware of it . . as you see. Our last conversation took in the end such a strange turn . . I did not want to part from you without expressing my sincere good feeling for you.'

'You have good feeling for me now . . . when I am going away?'

Potugin looked mournfully at Litvinov. 'Ah, Grigory Mihalitch, Grigory Mihalitch,' he began with a short sigh, 'it's no time for that with us now, no time for delicacy or fencing. You don't, so far as I have been able to perceive, take much interest in our national literature, and so, perhaps, you have no clear conception of Vaska Buslaev?'

'Of whom?'

'Of Vaska Buslaev, the hero of Novgorod . . . in Kirsch-Danilov's collection.'

'What Buslaev?' said Litvinov, somewhat puzzled by the unexpected turn of the conversation. 'I don't know.'

'Well, never mind. I only wanted to draw your attention to something. Vaska Buslaev, after he had taken away his Novgorodians on a pilgrimage to Jerusalem, and there, to their horror, bathed all naked in the holy river Jordan, for he believed not "in omen nor in dream, nor in the flight of birds," this logical Vaska Buslaev climbed up Mount Tabor, and on the top of this mountain there lies a great stone, over which men of every kind have tried in vain to jump. . . . Vaska too ventured to try his luck. And he chanced upon a dead head, a human skull in his road; he kicked it away with his foot. So the skull said to him; "Why do you kick me? I knew how to live, and I know how to roll in the dust—and it will be the same with you." And in fact, Vaska jumps over the stone, and he did quite clear it, but he caught his heel and broke his skull. And in this place, I must by the way observe that it wouldn't be amiss for our friends, the Slavophils, who are so fond of kicking dead heads and decaying nationalities underfoot to ponder over that legend.'

'But what does all that mean?' Litvinov interposed impatiently at last. 'Excuse me, it's time for me . . .'

'Why, this,' answered Potugin, and his eyes beamed with such affectionate warmth as Litvinov had not even expected of him, 'this, that you do not spurn a dead human head, and for your goodness, perhaps you may succeed in leaping over the fatal stone. I won't keep you any longer, only let me embrace you at parting.'

'I'm not going to try to leap over it even,' Litvinov declared, kissing Potugin three times, and the bitter sensations filling his soul were replaced for an instant by pity for the poor lonely creature.

'But I must go, I must go. . . .' he moved about the room.

'Can I carry anything for you?' Potugin proffered his services.

'No, thank you, don't trouble, I can manage. . . .'

He put on his cap, took up his bag. 'So you say,' he queried, stopping in the doorway, 'you have seen her?'

'Yes, I've seen her.'

'Well . . . tell me about her.'

Potugin was silent a moment. 'She expected you yesterday . . . and to-day she will expect you.'

'Ah! Well, tell her . . . No, there's no need, no need of anything. Good-bye . . . Good-bye!'

'Good-bye, Grigory Mihalitch. . . . Let me say one word more to you. You still have time to listen to me; there's more than half an hour before the train starts. You are returning to

Russia . . . There you will . . . in time . . . get to work . . . Allow an old chatterbox—for, alas, I am a chatterbox, and nothing more—to give you advice for your journey. Every time it is your lot to undertake any piece of work, ask yourself: Are you serving the cause of civilisation, in the true and strict sense of the word; are you promoting one of the ideals of civilisation; have your labours that educating, Europeanising character which alone is beneficial and profitable in our day among us? If it is so, go boldly forward, you are on the right path, and your work is a blessing! Thank God for it! You are not alone now. You will not be a "sower in the desert"; there are plenty of workers . . . pioneers . . . even among us now . . . But you have no ears for this now. Good-bye, don't forget me!'

Litvinov descended the staircase at a run, flung himself into a carriage, and drove to the station, not once looking round at the town where so much of his personal life was left behind. He abandoned himself, as it were, to the tide; it snatched him up and bore him along, and he firmly resolved not to struggle against it . . . all other exercise of independent will he renounced.

He was just taking his seat in the railway carriage.

'Grigory Mihalitch ... Grigory ...' he heard a supplicating whisper behind him.

He started ... Could it be Irina? Yes; it was she. Wrapped in her maid's shawl, a travelling hat on her dishevelled hair, she was standing on the platform, and gazing at him with worn and weary eyes.

'Come back, come back, I have come for you,' those eyes were saying. And what, what were they not promising? She did not move, she had not power to add a word; everything about her, even the disorder of her dress, everything seeemed entreating forgiveness ...

Litvinov was almost beaten, scarcely could he keep from rushing to her ... But the tide to which he had surrendered himself reasserted itself. ... He jumped into the carriage, and turning round, he motioned Irina to a place beside him. She understood him. There was still time. One step, one movement, and two lives made one for ever would have been hurried away into the uncertain distance. ... While she wavered, a loud whistle sounded and the train moved off.

Litvinov sank back, while Irina moved staggering to a seat, and fell on it, to the immense astonishment of a supernumerary diplomatic official who chanced to be lounging about the railway station. He was slightly acquainted with Irina, and greatly admired her, and seeing that she lay as though overcome by faintness, he imagined that she had '*une attaque de nerfs*,' and therefore deemed it his duty, the duty *d'un galant chevalier*, to go to her assistance. But his astonishment assumed far greater proportions when, at the first word addressed to her, she suddenly got up, repulsed his proffered arm, and hurrying out into the street, had in a few instants vanished in the milky vapour of fog, so characteristic of the climate of the Black Forest in the early days of autumn.

XXVI

WE happened once to go into the hut of a peasant-woman who had just lost her only, passionately loved son, and to our considerable astonishment we found her perfectly calm, almost cheerful. 'Let her be,' said her husband, to whom probably our astonishment was apparent, 'she is gone numb now.' And Litvinov had in the same way 'gone numb.' The same sort of calm came over him during the first few hours of the journey. Utterly crushed, hopelessly wretched as he was, still he was at rest, at rest after the agonies and sufferings of the last few weeks, after all the blows which had fallen one after another upon his head. They had been the more shattering for him that he was little fitted by nature for such tempests. Now he really hoped for nothing, and tried not to remember, above all not to remember. He was going to Russia . . . he had to go somewhere; but he was making no kind of plans regarding his own personality. He did not recognise himself, he did not comprehend his own actions, he had positively lost his real identity, and, in fact, he took very little interest in his own identity. Sometimes it seemed to him that he was taking his own corpse home, and only the bitter spasms of irremediable spiritual pain passing over him from time to time brought him back to a sense of still being alive. At times it struck him as incomprehensible that a man—a man!—could let a woman, let love, have such power over him . . . 'Ignominious weakness!' he muttered, and shook back his cloak, and sat up more squarely; as though to say, the past is over, let's begin fresh . . . a moment, and he could only smile bitterly and wonder at himself. He fell to looking out of the window. It was grey and damp; there was no rain, but the fog still hung about; and low clouds trailed across the sky. The wind blew facing the train; whitish clouds of steam, some singly, others mingled with other darker clouds of smoke, whirled in endless file past the window at which Litvinov was sitting. He began to watch this steam, this smoke. Incessantly mounting, rising and falling, twisting and hooking on to the grass, to the bushes as though in sportive antics, lengthening out, and hiding away, clouds upon clouds flew by . . . they were for ever changing and stayed still the same in their monotonous, hurrying, wearisome sport! Sometimes the wind changed, the line bent to right or left, and suddenly the whole mass vanished, and at once reappeared at the opposite window; then again the huge tail was flung out, and again it veiled Litvinov's view of the vast plain of the Rhine. He gazed and gazed, and a strange reverie came over him . . . He was alone in the compartment; there was no one to disturb him. 'Smoke, smoke,' he repeated several times; and suddenly it all seemed as smoke to him, everything, his own life, Russian life—everything human, especially everything Russian. All smoke and steam, he thought; all seems for ever changing, on all sides new forms, phantoms flying after phantoms, while in reality it is all the same and the same again; everything hurrying, flying towards something, and everything vanishing without a trace, attaining to nothing; another wind blows, and all is dashing in the opposite direction, and there again the same untiring, restless—and useless gambols! He remembered much that had taken place with clamour and flourish before his eyes in the last few years . . . 'Smoke,' he whispered, 'smoke'; he remembered the hot disputes, the wrangling, the clamour at Gubaryov's, and in other sets of men, of high and low degree, advanced and reactionist, old and young . . . 'Smoke,' he repeated, 'smoke and steam'; he remembered, too, the fashionable picnic, and he remembered various opinions and speeches of other political personages —even all Potugin's sermonising . . . 'Smoke, smoke, nothing but smoke.' And what of his own struggles and passions and agonies and dreams? He could only reply with a gesture of despair.

And meanwhile the train dashed on and on; by now Rastadt, Carlsruhe, and Bruchsal had long been left far behind; the mountains on the right side of the line swerved aside, retreated into the distance, then moved up again, but not so high, and more thinly covered with trees. . . . The train made a sharp turn . . . and there was Heidelberg. The carriage rolled in under the cover of the station; there was the shouting of newspaper-boys, selling papers of all sorts, even Russian; passengers began bustling in their seats, getting out on to the platform, but Litvinov did not leave his corner, and still sat on with downcast head. Suddenly some one called him by name; he raised his eyes; Bindasov's ugly phiz was thrust in at the window; and behind him—or was he dreaming, no, it was really so—all the familiar Baden faces;

there was Madame Suhantchikov, there was Voroshilov, and Bambaev too; they all rushed up to him, while Bindasov bellowed:

'But where's Pishtchalkin? We were expecting him; but it's all the same, hop out, and we'll be off to Gubaryov's.'

'Yes, my boy, yes, Gubaryov's expecting us,' Bambaev confirmed, making way for him, ' hop out.'

Litvinov would have flown into a rage, but for a dead load lying on his heart. He glanced at Bindasov and turned away without speaking.

'I tell you Gubaryov's here,' shrieked Madame Suhantchikov, her eyes fairly starting out of her head.

Litvinov did not stir a muscle.

'Come, do listen, Litvinov,' Bambaev began at last, 'there's not only Gubaryov here, there's a whole phalanx here of the most splendid, most intellectual young fellows, Russians—and all studying the natural sciences, all of the noblest convictions! Really you must stop here, if it's only for them. Here, for instance, there's a certain . . . there, I've forgotten his surname, but he's a genius! simply!'

'Oh, let him be, let him be, Rostislav Ardalionovitch,' interposed Madame Suhantchikov, 'let him be! You see what sort of a fellow he is; and all his family are the same. He has an aunt; at first she struck me as a sensible woman, but the day before yesterday I went to see her here—she had only just before gone to Baden and was back here again before you could look round—well, I went to see her; began questioning her . . Would you believe me, I couldn't get a word out of the stuck-up thing. Horrid aristocrat!'

Poor Kapitolina Markovna an aristocrat! Could she ever have anticipated such a humiliation?

But Litvinov still held his peace, turned away, and pulled his cap over his eyes. The train started at last.

'Well, say something at parting at least, you stonyhearted man!' shouted Bambaev, 'this is really too much!'

'Rotten milksop!' yelled Bindasov. The carriages were moving more and more rapidly, and he could vent his abuse with impunity. 'Niggardly stick-in-the-mud.'

Whether Bindasov invented this last appellation on the spot, or whether it had come to him second-hand, it apparently gave great satisfaction to two of the noble young fellows studying natural science, who happened to be standing by, for only a few days later it appeared in the Russian periodical sheet, published at that time at Heidelberg under the title: *A tout venant je crache!*[1] or, 'We don't care a hang for anybody!'

But Litvinov repeated again, 'Smoke, smoke, smoke! Here,' he thought, 'in Heidelberg now are over a hundred Russian students; they're all studying chemistry, physics, physiology—they won't even hear of anything else . . . but in five or six years' time there won't be fifteen at the lectures by the same celebrated professors; the wind will change, the smoke will be blowing . . . in another quarter . . . smoke . . . smoke . . . !'[2]

Towards nightfall he passed by Cassel. With the darkness intolerable anguish pounced like a hawk upon him, and he wept, burying himself in the corner of the carriage. For a long time his tears flowed, not easing his heart, but torturing him with a sort of gnawing bitterness; while at the same time, in one of the hotels of Cassel, Tatyana was lying in bed feverishly ill.

Kapitolina Markovna was sitting beside her. 'Tanya,' she was saying, 'for God's sake, let

---

[1] A historical fact.

[2] Litvinov's presentiments came true. In 1866 there were in Heidelberg thirteen Russian students entered for the summer, and twelve for the winter session.

me send a telegram to Grigory Mihalitch, do let me, Tanya!'

'No, aunt,' she answered; 'you mustn't; don't be frightened, give me some water; it will soon pass.'

And a week later she did, in fact, recover, and the two friends continued their journey.

XXVII

STOPPING neither at Petersburg nor at Moscow, Litvinov went back to his estate. He was dismayed when he saw his father; the latter was so weak and failing. The old man rejoiced to have his son, as far as a man can rejoice who is just at the close of life; he at once gave over to him the management of everything, which was in great disorder, and lingering on a few weeks longer, he departed from this earthly sphere. Litvinov was left alone in his ancient little manor-house, and with a heavy heart, without hope, without zeal, and without money, he began to work the land. Working the land is a cheerless business, as many know too well; we will not enlarge on how distasteful it seemed to Litvinov. As for reforms and innovations, there was, of course, no question even of them; the practical application of the information he had gathered abroad was put off for an indefinite period; poverty forced him to make shift from day to day, to consent to all sorts of compromises—both material and moral. The new had 'begun ill,' the old had lost all power; ignorance jostled up against dishonesty; the whole agrarian organisation was shaken and unstable as quagmire bog, and only one great word, 'freedom,' was wafted like the breath of God over the waters. Patience was needed before all things, and a patience not passive, but active, persistent, not without tact and cunning at times. . . . For Litvinov, in his frame of mind, it was doubly hard. He had but little will to live left in him. . . . Where was he to get the will to labour and take trouble?

But a year passed, after it another passed, the third was beginning. The mighty idea was being realised by degrees, was passing into flesh and blood, the young shoot had sprung up from the scattered seed, and its foes, both open and secret, could not stamp it out now. Litvinov himself, though he had ended by giving up the greater part of his land to the peasants on the half-profit system, that's to say, by returning to the wretched primitive methods, had yet succeeded in doing something; he had restored the factory, set up a tiny farm with five free hired labourers—he had had at different times fully forty—and had paid his principal private debts. . . . And his spirit had gained strength; he had begun to be like the old

Litvinov again. It's true, a deeply buried melancholy never left him, and he was too quiet for his years; he shut himself up in a narrow circle and broke off all his old connections ... but the deadly indifference had passed, and among the living he moved and acted as a living man again. The last traces, too, had vanished of the enchantment in which he had been held; all that had passed at Baden appeared to him dimly as in a dream. . . . And Irina? even she had paled and vanished too, and Litvinov only had a faint sense of something dangerous behind the mist that gradually enfolded her image. Of Tatyana news reached him from time to time; he knew that she was living with her aunt on her estate, a hundred and sixty miles from him, leading a quiet life, going out little, and scarcely receiving any guests—cheerful and well, however. It happened on one fine May day, that he was sitting in his study, listlessly turning over the last number of a Petersburg paper; a servant came to announce the arrival of an old uncle. This uncle happened to be a cousin of Kapitolina Markovna and had been recently staying with her. He had bought an estate in Litvinov's vicinity and was on his way thither. He stayed twenty-four hours with his nephew and told him a great deal about Tatyana's manner of life. The next day after his departure Litvinov sent her a letter, the first since their separation. He begged for permission to renew her acquaintance, at least by correspondence, and also desired to learn whether he must for ever give up all idea of some day seeing her again? Not without emotion he awaited the answer . . . the answer came at last. Tatyana responded cordially to his overture. 'If you are disposed to pay us a visit,' she finished up, 'we hope you will come; you know the saying, "even the sick are easier together than apart."' Kapitolina Markovna joined in sending her regards. Litvinov was as happy as a child; it was long since his heart had beaten with such delight over anything. He felt suddenly light and bright. . . . Just as when the sun rises and drives away the darkness of night, a light breeze flutters with the sun's rays over the face of the reviving earth. All that day Litvinov kept smiling, even while he went about his farm and gave his orders. He at once began making arrangements for the journey, and a fortnight later he was on his way to Tatyana.

XXVIII

HE drove rather slowly by cross tracks, without any special adventures; only once the tire of a hind wheel broke; a blacksmith hammered and welded it, swearing both at the tire and at himself, and positively flung up the job; luckily it turned out that among us one can travel capitally even with a tire broken, especially on the 'soft,' that's to say on the mud. On the other hand, Litvinov did come upon some rather curious chance-meetings. At one place he found a Board of Mediators sitting, and at the head of it Pishtchalkin, who made on him the impression of a Solon or a Solomon, such lofty wisdom characterised his remarks, and such boundless respect was shown him both by landowners and peasants. . . . In exterior, too, he had begun to resemble a sage of antiquity; his hair had fallen off the crown of his head, and his full face had completely set in a sort of solemn jelly of positively blatant virtue. He expressed his pleasure at

Litvinov's arrival in—'if I may make bold to use so ambitious an expression, my own district,' and altogether seemed fairly overcome by an excess of excellent intentions. One piece of news he did, however, succeed in communicating, and that was about Voroshilov; the hero of the Golden Board had re-entered military service, and had already had time to deliver a lecture to the officers of his regiment on Buddhism or Dynamism, or something of the sort—Pishtchalkin could not quite remember. At the next station it was a long while before the horses were in readiness for Litvinov; it was early dawn, and he was dozing as he sat in his coach. A voice, that struck him as familiar, waked him up; he opened his eyes.... Heavens! wasn't it Gubaryov in a grey pea-jacket and full flapping pyjamas standing on the steps of the posting hut, swearing?... No, it wasn't Mr. Gubaryov.... But what a striking resemblance!... Only this worthy had a mouth even wider, teeth even bigger, the expression of his dull eyes was more savage and his nose coarser, and his beard thicker, and the whole countenance heavier and more repulsive.

'Scou-oundrels, scou-oundrels!' he vociferated slowly and viciously, his wolfish mouth gaping wide. 'Filthy louts.... Here you have ... vaunted freedom indeed ... and can't get horses ... scou-oundrels!'

'Scou-oundrels, scou-oundrels!' thereupon came the sound of another voice from within, and at the same moment there appeared on the steps—also in a grey smoking pea-jacket and pyjamas—actually, unmistakably, the real Gubaryov himself, Stepan Nikolaevitch Gubaryov. 'Filthy louts!' he went on in imitation of his brother (it turned out that the first gentleman was his elder brother, the man of the old school, famous for his fists, who had managed his estate). 'Flogging's what they want, that's it; a tap or two on the snout, that's the sort of freedom for them. ... Self-government indeed. ... I'd let them know it. ... But where is that M'sieu Roston? ... What is he thinking about? ... It's his business, the lazy scamp ... to see we're not put to inconvenience.'

'Well, I told you, brother,' began the elder Gubaryov, 'that he was a lazy scamp, no good in fact! But there, for the sake of old times, you ... M sieu Roston, M'sieu Roston! ... Where have you got to?'

'Roston! Roston!' bawled the younger, the great Gubaryov. 'Give a good call for him, do brother Dorimedont Nikolaitch!'

'Well, I am shouting for him, Stepan Nikolaitch! M'sieu Roston!'

'Here I am, here I am, here I am!' was heard a hurried voice, and round the corner of the hut skipped Bambaev.

Litvinov fairly gasped. On the unlucky enthusiast a shabby braided coat, with holes in the elbows, dangled ruefully; his features had not exactly changed, but they looked pinched and drawn together; his over-anxious little eyes expressed a cringing timorousness and hungry servility; but his dyed whiskers stood out as of old above his swollen lips. The Gubaryov brothers with one accord promptly set to scolding him from the top of the steps; he stopped, facing them below, in the mud, and with his spine curved deprecatingly, he tried to propitiate them with a little nervous smile, kneading his cap in his red fingers, shifting from one foot to the other, and muttering that the horses would be here directly.... But the brothers did not cease, till the younger at last cast his eyes upon Litvinov. Whether he recognised Litvinov, or whether he felt ashamed before a stranger, anyway he turned abruptly on his heels like a bear, and gnawing his beard, went into the station hut; his brother held his tongue at once, and he too, turning like a bear, followed him in. The great Gubaryov, evidently, had not lost his influence even in his own country.

Bambaev was slowly moving after the brothers.... Litvinov called him by his name. He looked round, lifted up his head, and recognising Litvinov, positively flew at him with outstretched arms; but when he had run up to the carriage, he clutched at the carriage door, leaned over it, and began sobbing violently.

'There, there, Bambaev,' protested Litvinov, bending over him and patting him on the shoulder.

But he went on sobbing. 'You see ... you see ... to what ...' he muttered brokenly.

'Bambaev!' thundered the brothers from the hut.

Bambaev raised his head and hurriedly wiped his tears.

'Welcome, dear heart,' he whispered, 'welcome and farewell!... You hear, they are calling me.'

'But what chance brought you here?' inquired Litvinov, 'and what does it all mean? I thought they were calling a Frenchman....'

'I am their ... house-steward, butler,' answered Bambaev, and he pointed in the direction of the hut. 'And I'm turned Frenchman for a joke. What could I do, brother? You see, I'd nothing to eat, I'd lost my last farthing, and so one's forced to put one's head under the yoke. One can't afford to be proud.'

'But has he been long in Russia? and how did he part from his comrades?'

'Ah, my boy, that's all on the shelf now. ... The wind's changed, you see. ... Madame Suhantchikov, Matrona Semyonovna, he simply kicked out. She went to Portugal in her grief.'

'To Portugal? How absurd!'

'Yes, brother, to Portugal, with two Matronovtsys.'

'With whom?'

'The Matronovtsys; that's what the members of her party are called.'

'Matrona Semyonovna has a party of her own? And is it a numerous one?'

'Well, it consists of precisely those two. And he will soon have been back here six months. Others have got into difficulties, but he was all right. He lives in the country with his brother, and you should just hear him now...'

'Bambaev!'

'Coming, Stepan Nikolaitch, coming. And you, dear old chap, are flourishing, enjoying yourself! Well, thank God for that! Where are you off to now?... There, I never thought, I never guessed.... You remember Baden? Ah, that was a place to live in! By the way, you remember Bindasov too? Only fancy, he's dead. He turned exciseman, and was in a row in a public-house; he got his head broken with a billiard-cue. Yes, yes, hard times have come now! But still I say, Russia . . . ah, our Russia! Only look at those two geese; why, in the whole of Europe there's nothing like them! The genuine Arzamass breed!'

And with this last tribute to his irrepressible desire for enthusiasm, Bambaev ran off to the station hut, where again, seasoned with opprobrious epithets, his name was shouted.

Towards the close of the same day, Litvinov was nearly reaching Tatyana's village. The little house where his former betrothed lived stood on the slope of a hill, above a small river, in the midst of a garden recently planted. The house, too, was new, lately built, and could be seen a long way off across the river and the open country. Litvinov caught sight of it more than a mile and a half off, with its sharp gable, and its row of little windows, gleaming red in the evening sun. At starting from the last station he was conscious of a secret agitation; now he was in a tremor simply—a happy tremor, not unmixed with dread. 'How will they meet me?' he thought, 'how shall I present myself?' . . . To turn off his thoughts with something, he began talking with his driver, a steady peasant with a grey beard, who charged him, however, for twenty-five miles, when the distance was not twenty. He asked him, did he know the Shestov ladies?

'The Shestov ladies? To be sure! Kind-hearted ladies, and no doubt about it! They doctor us too. It's the truth I'm telling you. Doctors they are! People go to them from all about. Yes, indeed. They fairly crawl to them. If any one, take an example, falls sick, or cuts himself or anything, he goes straight to them and they'll give him a lotion directly, or powders, or a plaster, and it'll be all right, it'll do good. But one can't show one's gratitude, we won't consent to that, they say; it's not for money. They've set up a school too. . . . Not but what that's a foolish business!'

While the driver talked, Litvinov never took his eyes off the house. . . . Out came a woman in white on to the balcony, stood a little, stood and then disappeared. . . . 'Wasn't it she?' His heart was fairly bounding within him. 'Quicker, quicker!' he shouted to the driver; the latter urged on the horses. A few instants more . . . and the carriage rolled in through the opened gates. . . . And on the steps Kapitolina Markovna was already standing, and beside herself with joy, was clapping her hands crying, 'I heard him, I knew him first! It's he! it's he! . . I knew him!'

Litvinov jumped out of the carriage, without giving the page who ran up time to open the door, and hurriedly embracing Kapitolina Markovna, dashed into the house, through the hall, into the dining-room. . . . Before him, all shamefaced, stood Tatyana. She glanced at him with her kind caressing eyes (she was a little thinner, but it suited her), and gave him her hand. But he did not take her hand, he fell on his knees before her. She had not at all expected this and did not know what to say, what to do. . . . The tears started into her eyes. She was frightened, but her whole face beamed with delight. . . . 'Grigory Mihalitch, what is this, Grigory Mihalitch?' she said . . . while he still kissed the hem of her dress . . . and with a thrill of tenderness he recalled that at Baden he had been in the same way on his knees before her. . . . But then—and now!

'Tanya!' he repeated, 'Tanya! you have forgiven me, Tanya!'

'Aunt, aunt, what is this?' cried Tatyana turning to Kapitolina Markovna as she came in.

'Don't hinder him, Tanya,' answered the kind old lady. 'You see the sinner has repented.'

But it is time to make an end; and indeed there is nothing to add; the reader can guess the rest by himself. . . . But what of Irina?

She is still as charming, in spite of her

thirty years; young men out of number fall in love with her, and would fall in love with her even more, if . . . if . . .

Reader, would you care to pass with us for a few instants to Petersburg into one of the first houses there? Look; before you is a spacious apartment, we will not say richly—that is too low an expression—but grandly, imposingly, inspiringly decorated. Are you conscious of a certain flutter of servility? Know that you have entered a temple, a temple consecrated to the highest propriety, to the loftiest philanthropy, in a word, to things unearthly. . . . A kind of mystic, truly mystic, hush enfolds you. The velvet hangings on the doors, the velvet curtains on the window, the bloated, spongy rug on the floor, everything as it were destined and fitted beforehand for subduing, for softening all coarse sounds and violent sensations. The carefully hung lamps inspire well-regulated emotions; a discreet fragrance is diffused in the close air; even the samovar on the table hisses in a restrained and modest manner. The lady of the house, an important personage in the Petersburg world, speaks hardly audibly; she always speaks as though there were some one dangerously ill, almost dying in the room; the other ladies, following her example, faintly whisper; while her sister, pouring out tea, moves her lips so absolutely without sound that a young man sitting before her, who has been thrown by chance into the temple of decorum, is positively at a loss to know what she wants of him, while she for the sixth time breathes to him, '*Voulez-vous une tasse de thé?*' In the corners are to be seen young, good-looking men; their glances are brightly, gently ingratiating; unruffled gentleness, tinged with obsequiousness, is apparent in their faces; a number of the stars and crosses of distinction gleam softly on their breasts. The conversation is always gentle; it turns on religious and patriotic topics, the Mystic Drop, F. N. Glinka, the missions in the East, the monasteries and brotherhoods in White Russia. At times, with muffled tread over the soft carpets, move footmen in livery; their huge calves, cased in tight silk stockings, shake noiselessly at every step; the respectful motion of the solid muscles only augments the general impression of decorum, of solemnity, of sanctity.

It is a temple, a temple!

'Have you seen Madame Ratmirov to-day?' one great lady queries softly.

'I met her to-day at Lise's,' the hostess answers with her Æolian note. 'I feel so sorry for her. . . . She has a satirical intellect . . . *elle n'a pas la foi.*'

'Yes, yes,' repeats the great lady . . . 'that

I remember, Piotr Ivanitch said about her, and very true it is, *qu'elle a . . . qu'elle a* an ironical intellect.'

'*Elle n'a pas la foi,*' the hostess's voice exhaled like the smoke of incense,—'*C'est une âme égarée.* She has an ironical mind.'

And that is why the young men are not all without exception in love with Irina. . . . They are afraid of her . . . afraid of her 'ironical intellect.' That is the current phrase about her; in it, as in every phrase, there is a grain of truth. And not only the young men are afraid of her; she is feared by grown men too, and by men in high places, and even by the grandest personages. No one can so truly and artfully scent out the ridiculous or petty side of a character, no one else has the gift of stamping it mercilessly with the never-forgotten word. . . . And the sting of that word is all the sharper that it comes from lovely, sweetly fragrant lips. . . . It's hard to say what passes in that soul; but in the crowd of her adorers rumour does not recognise in any one the position of a favoured suitor.

Irina's husband is moving rapidly along the path which among the French is called the path of distinction. The stout general has shot past him; the condescending one is left behind.

And in the same town in which Irina lives, lives also our friend Sozont Potugin; he rarely sees her, and she has no special necessity to keep up any connection with him. . . . The little girl who was committed to his care died not long ago.

THE END

Printed by T. and A. CONSTABLE, Printers to His Majesty, at the Edinburgh University Press

www.ingramcontent.com/pod-product-compliance
Lightning Source LLC
Chambersburg PA
CBHW030010240426
43672CB00007B/899